———

GROWING UP
AT ANY AGE

GROWING UP AT ANY AGE

How To Know When True Adulthood Arrives

Steven K. Baum, Ph.D.

Health Communications, Inc.
Deerfield Beach, Florida

Library of Congress Cataloging-in-Publication Data

Baum, Steven K.
    Growing up at any age: how to know when true adulthood
arrives/Steven K Baum.
        p.   cm.
    Includes bibliographical references.
    ISBN 1-55874-292-1 (pbk.): $9.95
    1. Emotional maturity. 2. Adulthood — Psychological as-
pects. 3. Aging — Psychological aspects. I. Title.
BF710.B39   1994   93-50846
155.2'5—dc20   CIP

©1994 Steven K. Baum
ISBN 1-55874-292-1

Publisher: Health Communications, Inc.
               3201 S.W. 15th Street
               Deerfield Beach, FL 33442-8190

Cover design by Robert Cannata

To
Joel Sekely,
and others who
exemplify wisdom and
compassion

Timeless Thoughts On Growing Up

*Man plays only when he is in the
full sense of the word a man, and wholly
a man when he is playing.*
— Friedrich Schiller

• • • • • •

*The maturity of man is said to have acquired
the sensuousness of a child at play.*
— Friedrich Nietzsche

• • • • • •

*Life is not too short for those
who use it wisely.*
— Seneca

• • • • • •

*Anyone who keeps the ability to
see beauty is not old.*
— Franz Kafka

• • • • • •

*As long as one can admire and love
then one is young forever.*
— Pablo Casals

• • • • • •

*Man unlike the animals has never learned that
the sole purpose of life is to enjoy it.*
— Sam Butler

• • • • • •

*Well the trick is simple —
to die young as late as possible.*
— Ashley Montagu

*You grow up the day you have the
first real laugh at yourself.*
— Ethel Barrymore

• • • • • •

*As you grow up, you'll find that the
only things you regret are the
things you didn't do.*
— Mildred Pierce

• • • • • •

*As long as you can still be
disappointed, you are still young.*
— Sarah Churchill

• • • • • •

*I think age is a high price
to pay for maturity.*
— Tom Stoppard

• • • • • •

*Some of our greatest scientists and
musicians from Einstein to Mozart appear
to have been exceptionally neotenous.
People always say, "He may be like a child."
They don't realize that perhaps being like
a child is what made him great!*
— Richard Cutler

• • • • • •

*In all major myths and religions, the same theme occurs:
A hero ventures forth into a region of supernatural wonder.
Forces are encountered and victory is won.
The hero returns with the power to
bestow boons on his fellow man.*
— Joseph Campbell

ACKNOWLEDGMENTS

I'd like to thank those who were kind, wise or helpful along the way. Thanks to Mary Linda Murphy, who stood by me and believed in what I was doing.

Thanks to Health Communications' editorial director Barbara Nichols, a kindred spirit who made the appalling process of publishing in the 1990s a little more humane. And to Jack Vitek for his masterful copy editing.

In the Detroit-Windsor area: I'd like to thank Hy and Rita Muroff, J. K. and Eve, Jack, Sylvia and Betty Baum, Irwin and Ruth Kahn, Elaine Greene, Don, Mindy, Howard and the Burkes, Paul and Paris Nesseth, R.J. Silver, Howard Lampe, Danny Winbaum, Lisa and Alan Isaacs, Beverly Darrenkamp and Robbie Stewart, Louise Centers, Barbara Klont, Pattie Riley, Pat and Carol Ann Duronio, Diana Trivax and Becky, Kenneth Carte, Ron Stearn, Ezil Braceful, Diane Shelby, Bruce Jerris, Bruce Levine, Allen Starr, Lauree and Bill Autterson, Theresa and John Smith,

Christi Bellino, Julie Hunt, Darlene Bacynski, Annette Sherry, Beth Nutter, Jeff Witek, Shirl Yoas, Jo Yaklin, Valerie Thompson, Art Hughett, Bridget Peterson, Erick Olsen, George Shiffer, Sharon Huth, Susan B. Smith, Alex McKee, Allen Pailleo, Jan Williams, Jane Zemba, Anne E. and Carol Cunningham, Ilene Thall and the incredibly helpful staff at the Baldwin Public Library, Birmingham, Michigan.

In Toronto: Thanks to Vince Valimbeek (psychic extraordinaire), Jim Seltz, Patty Muroff, Marcia Sokolowski, Donald Young, Otto Weininger, Steven, Ricki, Helen and Mark Sharpe, Chunkie Winbaum, Larry Goldin, Paul Gellman, Bonnie L. Croll, Jimmy Heller, Camp Kawagama.

In Los Angeles: Thanks to Morris Paulson, Randy Norris, David Aronson, Diana Taylor, Russell Boxley, Bea Daccardi and Carrie, Laurence and Toni Dworet, Art and Margie Fine and Denise and Bob Hanisee, Herb and Lillian, Rachel, Irwin, Josh, Aaron Willis, Frank and Marisa and Bob and Bobby Baum with special fondness to Ginette "Ketzie" Baum.

In the Bay area: Thanks to Mighty Joe Hindin, Karen Faith Tabachnick, Peter B. Gillman and Sharon.

I am grateful for critiques by Gloria Nixon-John, Doug Brown, Mintzi Schramm and thoughtfulness by Colin Ingram. Thanks also to Irma Turtle, Betty Conrades, Mindy Murphy, Bryan Murphy, Bizby, Jordan, Shaina, Josh, Elizabeth.

In memory of Poonam Shivastiva, Brian Caldwell, Mark Lawrence, the 1.6 million children of the Holocaust and the others who never had the chance to become adults.

CONTENTS

Part II: Agelessness

Part III: Aging

INTRODUCTION

When and how do we become true adults? It is when we reach adulthood emotionally. The metamorphosis from childhood into adulthood in the emotional sense is not achieved at a set age. We may become adults physically at puberty, or legally at age twenty-one, but crossing these thresholds does not equate with the attainment of true adulthood, or emotional adulthood. Chronological adulthood and emotional adulthood are, indeed, two distinct worlds.

The transition to true adulthood is almost always accompanied by an emotional or physical crisis. The triggers can be as disparate as a near-death experience, a crucial birthday, giving birth, a career change, getting fired, a divorce, separation or the death of a loved one. This is a time when many people seek therapy — or get a divorce. And sometimes a belated transition into adulthood is what the much-discussed midlife crisis is really all about. But for most people this crisis comes earlier, usually in their early thirties.

As a clinical psychologist, I discovered that the shift leading to emotional adulthood occurs only once in a lifetime. After it begins, it rarely slows down, and it is never reversible. The emotional upheaval takes two to four years and like many emotional processes is difficult to describe in words.

The process brings up strong and tumultuous emotions — the horrors and terrors of depression and anxiety — and forces us to face hard truths about ourselves. We confront the fear of losing our old selves and cast away long-held definitions and dreams of adulthood. We become temporarily disillusioned and feel deeply isolated. Cultures around the globe often ceremonially re-create or mimic the ordeal, and sometimes the isolation, in coming-of-age rituals.

During the transition, we learn to focus on our true needs and interests, rather than those prescribed for us by society or our parents. With the realization that the fulfillment of these unique needs will result in the achievement of our life's purpose, we may become disinterested in conventional definitions of maturity. Instead, we decide to reach our goal by our own design. The very fact that we have the courage to do so signals our maturity.

Once we arrive at true adulthood, we will never really grow old. Paradoxically, that doddering and infirm state seems to be reserved for those who never really grew up.

I have found that the circumstances of the transition may vary from person to person, but the stories of achieving true adulthood are amazingly similar. People who felt old and sluggish, people who felt they were losing control over their lives, people who felt they were no longer in touch with their inner feelings, eventually transformed themselves into strong, able individuals. Many were surprised how easily they were able to re-establish contact with their core desires and beliefs and determine what mattered to them. Some surged forward, rediscovering strengths they had almost forgotten; others moved tentatively, trembling with fear. All reached emotional adulthood when they connected with a true sense of self, despite contrasting outside opinions.

This metamorphosis into adulthood always involves a crisis, but unlike many other crises, the outcome always involves a change for the better. As writer Mark Gerzon says, "The real crisis may hit those who don't change."

If you or a loved one is experiencing change, this book will explain what has been happening to you, and tell you what more to expect. You will also discover some unconventional and perhaps profound ideas to help you on the road to emotional adulthood.

This book falls into three sections — true adulthood, agelessness and aging — all central ideas for understanding emotional growth. The first part examines the impact of society's "age game" on our lives. Our current understanding of adulthood is enhanced through the views of experts in gerontology, lifespan psychology and adulthood research. The essence of adulthood is probed and tests are presented to help you determine the state of your own adulthood, along with reasons why some people never become true adults.

The section on agelessness introduces the concept of an "age-free" existence. After examining concepts of emotional youngness and oldness, we begin to understand there is no such thing as emotional old age and we can envision a sort of new world order of ageless living. We explore the changes occurring in response to a burgeoning population of age-free people.

The final section on aging describes how we can remain physically healthy and balanced in mind and body. I present the most recent advances in medicine, psychology and physiology to help you grow up without necessarily growing old.

As we become true, emotional adults, to what extent should we adhere to the dictates of society? Can we fit into society without bowing to all of its demands? Can we free ourselves from stereotypes and move toward a healthier, happier, more meaningful existence? Can we become free of the emotional confines of chronological age?

If you are beginning the shift toward true adulthood, this book may cause you to stop and contemplate the possibility of seeing life differently. It could be the trigger that will send you into your own chrysalis, causing you to lose sleep and walk around with your head in a fog for what might seem an endless period. But after weeks, months or possibly even years, you will emerge on the other side feeling more stable than ever before. You will be an adult — for the very first time in your life — and you'll achieve a much better understanding of who you are and where you want to go.

If you are ready for a new and profound adventure, if you are open to the idea that you may have been culturally railroaded into accepting limits that have nothing to do with you as a person, then read on. You will find support for feelings you have had for a long time but didn't know were valid. You will discover how to set your spirit free in a culture that tries to block the spirit at every turn. You will discover that to grow up means more than submitting to socially and economically prescribed setpoints. You will discover how to grow up — at any age.

PART I:

TRUE ADULTHOOD

1

Adulthood: What Is It? Where Is It?

I don't think I've
ever felt like a grown-up.

*I think that I'm playing a grown-up
and that someday I might
be a grown-up.*

— Allen Funt, Age 78
Creator of *Candid Camera*

The Journey

Meet David, a university sociology professor: "I'm forty-two years old today, and I realize that I've only really been grown-up for a few months."

Meet Virginia, a seventy-two-year-old great-grandmother: "In my situation, having to raise my five children alone after my husband left me, I guess I never had the chance to figure out who I was. Even now that I'm raising my granddaughter, I still don't feel like an adult."

Meet Aung Trang, a thirty-one-year-old survivor of the Vietnam War: "I'm not sure, but I think I became a grown-up when I was eleven years old. My whole family was killed, but I escaped by walking through hundreds of miles of jungle, facing many dangers and constantly trying to find enough food to keep me alive. After that I didn't feel like a child any more. An adult? I don't know. It's just that I stopped being a child."

While most of us pass benchmarks that conventionally signal progress into adulthood, few of us may actually feel like adults. Doug, a colleague of mine in San Diego, illustrates the difference between the appearance and the actuality. At thirty-eight, his hair is slightly gray and there are a few lines on his face. He looks fully adult in his role as head of a child psychiatry program at a local hospital. He also acts the role. Married, with two children, he

4

works hard to support a lifestyle that will allow him to send his children to university and give them the extras in life. But what he says undercuts what he seems to be.

"I almost got fired again last week," he tells me with a note of panic. "I tried a political ploy that would have moved me up the hospital's corporate ladder. But I offended the wrong person."

Doug's careerism is not all that's wrong. Doug is so busy trying to master his fate and capture all the brass rings on the merry-go-round of life that he hasn't noticed the emotional distance developing between him and his wife. He doesn't see much of his children either, and he isn't quite sure what they're up to these days. He has yet to stop and ask himself the most crucial questions: Where is he going? What does it all mean?

Doug isn't alone. Millions of us get up every morning and plod through our daily routines. We leave for work or stay at home, meet with friends or deal with family, contribute to our block or complain about our neighbors. But we never take time to ask ourselves why. If Doug asks himself that question, he will probably begin to experience an emotional crisis that will launch the long transition to true adulthood.

It happened to me when I was twenty-nine. Fresh out of school, I was a young Pip right out of Charles Dickens's *Great Expectations* — naive, honest and without a clue about the way the working world operated. I landed a job at a large, urban hospital counseling center where I worked alongside three other junior psychologists and a menacing senior one. Our supervisor did not have our level of education, but he was far more streetwise. He was politically savvy and he was a bully. He continually threatened and criticized us, belittled our work and bragged about his. We worked in a clinical reign of terror.

"You'd better grow up, or I'll get some real staff in here," he would threaten. "You'll never amount to anything. Start acting like professionals — start acting like adults," he'd hammer away at us.

What he really meant was that we should give priority to our paperwork rather than our patients. He wanted us to attend meetings and present his department to good advantage. He was primarily interested in his own advancement.

As I look back, I wonder why I put up with him as long as I did. At first I thought it was the money. But even if my salary had somehow been immune to his threats, I doubt that I would have stood up to him. The answer, I know now, has more to do with my emotional immaturity than with economics.

It's ironic that by giving in to my supervisor's demands to grow up and act like an adult, I was doing the opposite. I had not yet developed my own set of internal standards of adulthood and because of my lack of experience in a work setting, I was unable to understand his territorial hostility and did not know how to establish boundaries or where to draw the line. Unfortunately, my supervisor did. He fired me for failing to adhere to his myopic priorities.

I was devastated. This was my first job, and I had failed. This was not the way adulthood was supposed to be. I had been in therapy earlier as part of my training and also to assist my adjustment to graduate student life and, later, to the working world. After I was fired, I re-entered therapy.

I came to realize that I had just paid the stiffest price for not playing office politics. I learned that I never would please everyone and that I could only become fully adult if I acknowledged my inner feelings. I also discovered that the crisis I was experiencing was not on society's timetable. It was too early to be called a midlife crisis and too severe to be dismissed as just a normal depression over being fired. This deepset crisis hinged, instead, on a crucial shift in my mindset.

A serious emotional crisis preceding the transition to

true adulthood is not uncommon. It's like the crisis we experience when we mourn the loss of a loved one, but instead we mourn our past selves and our wasted years. Just as death highlights what matters most, this crisis helps us focus on what is personally significant. As we tune into our own needs and interests, society's external standards seem less important.

What we achieve at the end of this crisis is a true adulthood that enriches our lives. We are energized and never grow old. But no one can become an adult without first going through a shift and a metamorphosis, a process of transformation.

Not everyone makes the transition into true adulthood. Many cannot make it without assistance. There are few statistics on patients' reasons for entering psychotherapy, but I would guess that this crisis in negotiating the transition to adulthood is one of the most common. As a clinical psychologist I have seen hundreds of patients who've sought help in the classic struggle to reach adulthood.

They enter my office with what looks like agitated depression. They wonder who they are. They have begun to question the values that have sustained them so far and the accomplishments they have worked so hard to attain. They talk about feeling empty. Their agitation is a fear of losing their old self and having no new self to replace it.

Few of us welcome major change. Turning from a caterpillar to a butterfly stirs up agonizing emotions and involves many disturbing decisions. My transition to true adulthood felt devastating at the time. During my metamorphosis, I faced some hard truths about myself — my cowardice and my inability to act on my own principles. Now, I look back and can put my emotional turmoil in perspective as growing pains that are part and parcel of formulating a total sense of self.

As we begin to look more closely at what it means to be an adult, there are several questions to ponder. What are the hallmarks of adulthood? Do certain kinds of feelings and reactions mark an adult? Does adulthood depend on an abundance of virtue? Or is it primarily how we act rather than how we think?

Does true adulthood come only through certain kinds of experiences, and does life offer everyone the chance to go through these kinds of painful, life-altering changes? If we don't go through these changes, what do we become as we age?

Remember childhood? Adolescence? Those times of intense experience and high passions seemed endless. They did end, but what took their place? Adulthood, or something else? What do we mean when we speak of true adulthood? When does it begin? What brings it on? Is it something good? Can we hasten its onset? Once attained, is it permanent? Do we all eventually become adults? What can we do to make true adulthood richer and more fulfilling?

Rather than ignore the transition to adulthood, are there ways our society could encourage and recognize it? Or are the factors that promote or hinder the transition too individual and complex to classify?

One way we can understand adulthood better is to see how our society and others view chronological age, and how we construct both formal and informal rites of passage as markers.

Birthdays are the most obvious markers we use for growing up. Ticking off these significant milestones, we can drive at sixteen, vote at eighteen and enter into contracts at twenty-one. We are supposed to launch our careers and families in our twenties, move up the ladder of success in our thirties, forties and fifties and retire happily in our sixties. Sociologists and psychologists have pat categories as well. They divide our lifespan into seven distinct phases: infancy (birth to two), childhood (three to twelve), adolescence (thirteen to nineteen), young adulthood (nineteen to thirty-five), middle age (thirty-six to sixty), maturity (sixty to eighty) and old age (eighty plus).

Most people have a difficult time fitting into these compartments. Adolescence may last well beyond nineteen. Attainment of adulthood is far from predictable and certainly not guaranteed at age nineteen. Old age doesn't always begin at eighty. Some people never feel old, while others are labeled as elderly while they're still in their sixties or even fifties.

I watched my much-loved grandfather enter forced retirement at sixty-five and change from a spry, bright man to a fumbling, doddering "old" person almost overnight. Grandpa was a workaholic and his work was over. He had accepted society's notion that his personal worth was vastly reduced. I continue to wonder how he would have fared if society had supported his creative urge to keep working instead of putting him out to pasture. From observing him and many others, I discovered it's important to disregard age stereotypes and instead look at an individual's emotional state.

As I began to grow interested in the field of gerontology, I asked one of my professors at the University of Southern California, "When does a person become old?" He offered textbook answers, quoting sociologists who had determined the conventional cookie-cutter age categories. The fact that their theories had little to do with the subjective experiences of my grandfather — and almost everyone else — didn't seem to interest him.

After I completed my studies in gerontology, I realized that other stages of life were also artificially constructed, as well as the host of complex social theories that made little sense in terms of individual subjective experience. So I asked another professor, "When does adulthood begin?"

He didn't have a clear answer either, but spent the rest of the class discussing the theories of adulthood first formulated by psychologist Erik Erikson. The general idea was that those who adjust to their circumstances are giving evidence of their adulthood. Supposedly these people are adults because they look and act like adults.

When I became fully trained in gerontology, I set out to explore the kinds of deep internal changes that happen in people's lives. The people I encountered found adulthood difficult to define. Some said they became adults when they were in their teens. Others didn't know if or when they had become adults. Still others who rigorously followed society's timetables offered shallow, conventional answers and many viewed the latter stages of that schedule with uncertainty and distaste.

Some sought counseling, feeling anxious and depressed. My professional colleagues believed these people were suffering from depressive disorders. I believed they might simply be crossing over into adulthood.

Old age was equally difficult to pinpoint. Those who were age-labeled as old did not necessarily fit the category. Some in their sixties, seventies and eighties were fully occupied and happy. Like the Little Prince in Antoine de Saint-Exupéry's timeless children's story, they had retained what was "essential to the heart" and remained in touch with their innermost feelings. Despite their physical appearance, they were ageless. Others felt old and used up while still in their thirties.

Increasingly, age labels do not fit. In today's changing economy more of us choose to work at all ages. An unexpected boon may be that age-free productivity makes us more age-free in other aspects of life. Young adults are running sophisticated businesses, and grandmothers are serving fast food and helping us redefine old age. Traditional notions of age-appropriate behavior are also being discarded. For example, we are readier to accept older women dating younger men and we are less willing to base our emotional life on traditional cultural definitions.

2

Culture
And
Life's Stages

——

*There's no such thing as a
grown-up person.*

— André Malraux

Historical Perspective

Western society's rigid, time-oriented, money-based and sometimes damaging views on aging are rooted in history and tradition. In Europe and America some 200 years ago, society treated people as adults as soon as they could work the land. People married young, had children early and quickly took their places in society. Many individuals did not live to see fifty. Many succumbed early to poor nutrition, infectious disease, dangerous animals and other hazards of their normal life.

Portraits of children in this era show little adults, garbed in adult clothing and displaying stern, sober, adultlike expressions. Childhood was not really an accepted life stage.

By the turn of this century, the situation had begun to change as grade school education became the norm. In 1938, with the passage of the Fair Labor Standards Act, the federal government outlawed child labor.

As the century progressed, a high school diploma became an important factor in the job market, and adolescence gained a recognized place on the road to adulthood.

The concept of middle age is a recent development related to the fact that as a society, by and large, we no longer live in extended families. Middle age is defined as the stage after our children grow up and leave the nest. In the ever-changing economy of the 1990s, however, that definition may need to be revised as more young people live at home, unable to afford to move out.

Social Security benefits are a relatively recent phenomenon and have contributed to a redefinition of old age as the time after retirement. The Social Security Act of 1935 arbitrarily designated age sixty-five as the end of one's working life. As a result, we are pigeonholed.

Current Attitudes

In a personal essay, recently widowed Joan Gould describes her life and her need to marry young:

> *I felt as if an expiration date had been stamped on my forehead: If I wasn't married by twenty-five, why then I'd never marry according to popular wisdom, and my precious virginity would shrivel into spinsterhood. No one I knew dreamed that it was possible to bear a first child after the age of thirty.*

Age stereotypes continue to haunt Donna, age thirty-four. After marrying and having children in her twenties, she returned to school to complete her master's degree in social work. Today, despite her many accomplishments, Donna is afraid of aging. She believes age is eroding what she believes to be her only asset — her physical looks:

> *I can work on my feelings and emotions, but I look in the mirror and see myself just getting older. If I left Richard, I've got to be honest, who would want me?*

Elaine, a thirty-seven-year-old neurologist who has been busy with her academic career, winning one fellowship after another, is less concerned with her physical appearance. But she faces countless prying questions that focus on her biological status. People ask: "Don't you want to be married?"; "Do you ever think about children?" and "Shouldn't you be done with school by now?" Each question underscores the fact that Elaine is growing older, that motherhood will soon be out of her reach.

In reality, menopause often brings relief. In *The Silent Passage*, best-selling author Gail Sheehy argues that there is a great deal of misinformation circulating about menopause and that if more women were comfortable discussing the process, they might discover the feeling of freedom it brings. Carolyn Heilbrun, a humanities professor at Columbia University who moonlights as a mystery writer under the pseudonym Amanda Cross, discovered this freedom after fifty. For her, it was the joy of no longer being a sex object and the possibility of new adventures:

> *Women have internalized what you could call the patriarchal idea of what women should be, that they should be attractive to men. . . . When we pass the age that this is possible, we figure out a way to live as ourselves and not as objects of the male gaze.*

Although the psychological impact of aging is often more devastating for women, men have their problems too. NBC News anchor Tom Brokaw described the perils of turning fifty in the *New York Times Magazine:*

> *At fifty you can no longer play the part of the brash young man making the daring moves, secure in the knowledge that if they don't work out, there will probably be other chances. Achievement is no cause for praise, it is expected. At fifty, you begin to examine the passbook of your life with a new urgency. Suddenly all those casual promissory notes of years gone by are overdue. Oh my God, I still haven't learned French. At age fifty, you believe you can still climb Mt. McKinley, but then why does your doctor react with an expression of bemused contempt? It's the male equivalent of the biological clock ticking away. A grandfather clock. This year, an unsettling number of friends have died or developed terminal illnesses.*

Society generally regards a man who still struggles to make a living at age sixty as a failure: the thirty-year-old can struggle but the sixty-year-old should not have to. Aging men who do not attain sufficient money, power and status are viewed as inferior and are generally spurred by women.

Other Cultures

The German philosopher Arthur Schopenhauer once said that the first forty years of life furnish the text and the remaining thirty supply the commentary. But what goes on elsewhere? In the West we are so accustomed to evaluating things by periods of time, our rites of passage are closely tied to age. It's easy to assume the entire world is governed by this same devotion to the clock, but that's simply not so.

In many other cultures adulthood arrives with a certain event rather than at a certain age, and the event is often tied to a series of rites and rituals. The rituals may vary, but the underlying theme is the same. The individual is isolated for a period that may range from a few weeks to a few years. He is tested and taught, and those who pass these ceremonies of endurance, skills or knowledge return to their tribes as adults.

My own initiation rite into emotional adulthood took me to strange and foreign lands that I always wanted to visit. As part of my personal search, I investigated other cultures in order to better grasp how rituals foster this psychological process.

Initiation rites can include physical and mental ordeals. Among the Dani and Yali tribes of Irian Jaya (Indonesian New Guinea), for example, men have historically achieved manhood by fighting battles with neighboring tribes. These days, mock conflicts and archery competitions substitute for those historic battles, but the champions still receive the time-honored penis gourd, decorative feathers and kina shells.

Over on the eastern side of the island, boys from ten to eighteen years of age become adults through physical scarring and a series of trials, similar to those of the Kau of Sudan. When I asked Jeff, a native of a Mindimbit village on the Upper Sepik River, why he would submit to having his back and arms painfully scarred, he replied: "This is an honor! Why would I not do this for my honor?" And when he turns twenty-one, he will leave his wife and children for six months and undergo a series of bleeding and laceration trials.

The village elder who performs the ceremony was amazed by my concern for safety. "I haven't lost a young man yet!" he answered confidently.

Jeff's counterpart in the Huli region of Papua New Guinea must leave his family and move into a bachelor hut in the jungle with several others. For several years, they will live apart and let their hair grow. After it has grown sufficiently and been elaborately coiffed, the Huli boy-turned-man will cut it off and preserve it as a wig to be donned for special occasions. Since the hair ceremonies do not occur annually and since not all members participate at the same time, it is possible for the tribe to have "boys" as old as seventeen and "men" as young as eleven.

Brazil's Xavante have similar initiation rites. Initiates live apart from the tribe in bachelor huts, where they learn to hunt and fish. When they are sufficiently accomplished, their adulthood is signaled by a pierced ear and a palm leaf sheath encircling the penis. They are now ready for sexual relationships.

Australia's aborigines take this symbolism one step further. They peel back the foreskin of the penis and cut the flesh below. If the boy moves or shows any fear during this physical trial, he is deemed not ready to become a man.

In Africa, Congolese Kota paint their children blue, the color of death, to mark the death of childhood and rebirth as an adult. In Mali, within the Dogon cliff-dwelling culture, hats are worn to mark the stages of life. Many of these rituals and customs seem linked to age, but in fact they are not. The people of these societies do not keep track of time as we do, and few understand what we mean by age.

Pacific rim cultures generally divide life into three stages: training, work and retirement. But there are no set ages at which these stages begin and end. In Hindu societies, stages are defined only in broad terms. The early training stage *(brahmachari)* is followed by a householder period *(grihastha)* identified by marriage and the earning of a living. The third stage, retirement *(vanaprastha)*, is distinguished by spiritual pursuits. Few, if any, attain a fourth stage *(sanyasi)* in which material goods are renounced completely for a life devoted entirely to union with God.

Native Americans and traditional Chinese equate age with wisdom. Older people are wiser, and aging is good. But these societies have no set time for the arrival of wisdom. The wise elders of the Mohawks are those who know the myths that perpetuate the culture and preserve the most valued elements of the tribe. Those who achieve the necessary degree of knowledge are accepted as elders. For Navajos, elderhood can be conferred as early as thirty — suggesting definition of age in terms of status rather than of a chronological age.

High in the Himalayan kingdom of Bhutan, age is linked to productivity and people are considered old when they can no longer work. I asked Sona, seventy-one, who dates his infirmities from age sixty, if he was old yet and how he had decided. "My body got old many years ago," he said. "I used to chop wood and plow the fields. It is very difficult for me to do this now."

In the same region, Jumijangchubdari, seventy, believes he became old at forty or forty-five: "My body just broke down. Now I spend most of my days in prayer."

Wut, a small, lean cannibal from a Mindimbit village in New Guinea, also judges his age by his ability to work. The other tribespeople estimate he is about eighty. Wut knows only that he has begun "to face the setting sun." But he cannot say when his oldness began, and in spite of his venerable chronological age, by village standards he is not labeled old because he can still work.

Baba, who lives in Indonesia's Sulewesi region, while younger than Wut, is not as fortunate. Cataracts cloud his vision, and he says he no longer feels strong. For him this feeling constitutes old age.

The inhabitants of the Trobiand Islands have no way at all to express the passage of time. When an object changes, it becomes something new and different. For instance, for yams, a staple of their diet, there are four different words — with no common root — for an early yam, an unripe one, a ripe one and an over-ripe one. Anthropologists have verified that the islanders are unaware of any connection between the same yam at its different stages. An unripe yam is, to them, a different object from a ripe one. Continuity through time, as we know it, apparently does not exist. Consequently, a Trobriand adult is not the same person as he was when a child.

In non-Westernized cultures, biology plays a significant role in marking stages of adulthood, with reproduction functioning as the internal alarm clock that signals the changes. For some African and Arab tribes, female circumcision, or removing a young girl's clitoris, controls sexual pleasure and ritualizes the onset of adulthood. This horrific practice continues and affects an estimated 80 million women.

For most cultures, the onset of menstruation distinguishes the adult woman from the girl. The Dyaks of Asia

isolate their young girls as soon as they begin to menstru-
ate. For one year, the girls live in a white cabin, eating
only white foods and wearing white clothing. The Ap-
aches, the Eshira of Gabon and certain New Guinean
tribes also practice rituals on this theme. The Bemba of
Zambia have a month-long *chisungu* initiation for their
young girls, during which secret names and special dances
or songs are passed on from one generation to another.

Mexican Catholic girls celebrate their adult status at
fifteen in the *quincianera* ceremony. "It's special," says Sarah,
who will wear a white bridal gown and march solemnly
down the aisle of her church. "It's a personal relationship
between you and God. Nothing can ever change that."

In parts of the Middle East, it is still not unusual to see
a just-married woman paraded through town, complete
with the bloodied sheets of the marriage bed serving as
positive proof of her genuine transition to a new stage of
adulthood.

Even the Kalahari Desert's !Kung, a group notable for
avoiding age classifications, distinguish between old and
young women. They use the suffix "na" to identify those
past menopause. Men in these male-oriented cultures, of
course, remain ageless.

Age-Oriented Cultures

In Western industrialized societies, we closely tie stages
of life to chronological age. Here, one of our adult rites of
passage is financial independence over time. Credit card
companies offer higher credit limits to the fiscally mature.
Washington Post columnist Richard Cohen recounts his
Western rite of passage:

> *Several years ago, my family gathered on Cape Cod for a*
> *weekend. My parents were there, my sister and her daughter*
> *too, two cousins and, of course, my wife, my son, and me.*
> *We ate at one of those restaurants where the menu is*

*scrawled on a blackboard held by a chummy waiter, and
we had a wonderful time. With dinner concluded, the waiter set the check down in the middle of the table. That's
when it happened. My father did not reach for the check. In
fact, my father did nothing. Conversation was continued.
Finally, it dawned on me. Me! I was supposed to pick up
the check. After all these years, after hundreds of restaurant
meals with my parents, after a lifetime of thinking of my
father as the one with the bucks, it had all changed. I
reached for the check and whipped out my American Express card. My view of myself was suddenly altered. With a
stroke of the pen, I was suddenly an adult!*

Paul, the youngest of three children, came from the
Midwest; his father was a doctor, a general practitioner,
and his mother a homemaker. Life, he thought, was supposed to unfold like a book, the kind you read by the fire
on a snowy day, page by numbered page. "When I married
Lori," he reports, "I was twenty-six, and in law school.
Because of my age I thought that getting married was the
next logical step, but I really didn't know what to look for
in a wife."

Lori, a law school classmate, became his friend, his lover
and then his wife. He relied on her to shape their relationship, and she did, but Paul wasn't satisfied. They divorced
soon after their marriage, and Paul realized he had not
been ready for this adult relationship.

Paul expected his life to match the expectations and
dreams encouraged by Western society. The discrepancy
between reality and fantasy sent him reeling. He felt be-
trayed. Like Tom, too many of us are unhappy and unful-
filled, racing throughout life with one eye on society's
timetable and another on the actions of those around us,
anxiously measuring our progress against the achievements of others.

We want the all-American dream — to establish ourselves in a career right after school, to get married and

have children early, to move ahead rapidly in our professions, to retire young, to die old and fulfilled.

In reality, only twenty-eight percent of all households achieve this kind of American dream. Half will divorce, one out of five families will report some kind of incest, and an even greater percentage of households will endure some form of spouse or child abuse.

In Western society, time is a dictator, commanding us to meetings, appointments and deadlines. We condemn those who fail to be on time and praise those whose lives run like clockwork. We look for ways to make time — and ways to kill it. We believe that time converts everyone into an adult. The stepping-off point can be sixteen, eighteen, twenty-one or thirty-five, depending on whether one uses as a criterion the legal age to drive, vote, drink alcohol or run for president.

We are so busy following society's agenda that we fail to realize how we program ourselves for unhappiness. We want to achieve our milestones by certain ages; but age, professional and social status, and materialism are poor standards of self-fulfillment and adulthood. We want to compete and emerge winners every time, but unless we possess the prodigious talent of Mozart, who completed his first musical composition at five, we never measure up. Meanwhile our compliance with society's demands and our unquestioning acceptance of definitions of success often translate into our marrying too young or settling for an unsatisfying career. As John, forty-eight, the oldest son of a middle-class Ohio family puts it:

> *I went all through medical school and didn't even want to be a doctor. I did it for my parents because they wanted me to be a doctor. I thought, "I owe this to them." I wish I had done it for me.*

Too many of us wind up doing what we do not want to do or choosing a career for all the wrong reasons. Our impatience to be successful adults leads us astray and financial responsibilities keep us trapped there. When society's timetable determines adulthood, the result, too often, is painful conflict and anxiety.

"I've never felt as old as I did when I was twenty-eight," says Lonnie, a claims investigator. Voted "most likely to succeed" in high school, Lonnie went to college and graduate school, but she did not get the kind of degree she wanted. Feeling herself getting older, she slid into a job with the city health department instead of pursuing her childhood dream of becoming a doctor. Her work became less and less satisfying, but she failed to see how, as an adult, she could give up a guaranteed career and excellent benefits to pursue a dream.

At the other end of the spectrum, society too frequently and arbitrarily determines when we are too old by considering only our chronological age. Donald, a sixty-three-year-old sales representative, is feeling that pressure: "I can't believe that they expect me to retire," he says of his company. "I can easily keep up with the rest of the men, but they want these aggressive young kids who are all pumped up and raring to go. And the market is such that they can get away with it."

Emotions Versus Culture

The stress created in living by society's rigid timetable can be unrelenting. To protect ourselves, we set up defenses, relegating our real needs and feelings to the background. A false self becomes our primary identity, complete with culturally sanctioned emotions. Somewhere along the way, that decoy self hardens, masking our true nature.

Themes in literature and the arts often portray the struggle to maintain one's soul. In *Long Days Journey Into Night*, playwright Eugene O'Neill writes, "None of us can help the things life has done to us. They're done before you realize it, and once they're done they make you do other things until at last everything comes between you and what you'd like to be, and you've lost your true self forever." Psychoanalyst Karen Horney called it simply *despair* and observed that the most surprising thing was that people went on living as if they were still in immediate contact with an alive, spontaneous center. This was the complaint of Suzanne (played by Meryl Streep) in the Mike Nichols' production of *Postcards From The Edge* — that in spite of fame and fortune and a movie star mother, she could not "feel her life." The movie was, of course, based on Carrie Fisher's bestseller.

We become responsible, conforming, committed, autonomous and practical (subverting ideals and minimizing emotions), as well as politically, socially and economically savvy — with a judgment call on corruptible, since the ends justify the means. We become so good at masquerading as adults that we actually delay emotional maturation. We choose the big prize behind Door No. 3: the big house, the luxurious car, money, status, style, power. We never give our inner selves a chance to feel what matters until it is "age-appropriate," at retirement — a culturally sanctioned period for living as we really wanted to live all along.

In Japan, "window sitters" join the ranks of the unemployed, but are permitted to come to the office and act as if they were employed. They are granted office space where they gaze out the window and shuffle papers in order not to lose face. Not surprisingly, these in-house unemployed have a high suicide rate, for their corporate identity has all but ended and their personal identity never even emerged.

Pico Iyer delineates Japan's rigid age classification system in *The Lady And The Monk*:

> *Age, therefore, was always stressed in Japan as much as it was downplayed in the U.S. (where, in California at least, a sixteen-year old girl often looked so much older than her*

age, and her forty-year-old mother so much younger, that mother and daughter truly did end up looking like sisters, as the soap ads promised). One reason Japanese generally asked one another as soon as they were introduced, "How old are you?" was station — a thirty-year-old was expected to defer to someone thirty-five and to have priority over someone twenty-five. But it was also, and relatedly, to give and enforce a sense of identity.

Yet in some Japanese circles it is understood that the integration of the *omote* (cultural) and *ura* (real and emotional) is what adulthood is all about.

True adulthood may be more easily attained in individual-based cultures (Australia, the U.S., Canada, and Western Europe). Harry Triandis's work at the University of Illinois suggests the world be divided into two basic types of cultures: individual-based and collective-concerned, the latter being characterized by less individual and more ethnocentric society with strong family and tribal loyalties.

To become a true adult in an individual-oriented culture like our own, we must each experience a transition crisis. The nature of this crisis is a reorientation of our thoughts and actions from those dictated by society to those we choose for ourselves. We know, unfortunately, that many people — perhaps the majority — never complete the transition to true adulthood.

What our culture does to us if we let it is unbelievable. What we do to ourselves is unfortunately just as unbelievable.

3

Growing Pains

—

It's triggered when they realize one day about 2:30 pm that they apparently devoted their entire life to doing something they hate.

— Dave Barry
from *Dave Barry Turns 40*

Adults — Who Came In?

E motional adulthood can be very much like an unrehearsed Three Stooges movie. In a classic routine, the Stooges would find themselves at a fancy society party. A butler would address them as "gentlemen," whereupon they would look around for the gentlemen in question, since they knew the butler couldn't possibly be talking to them. Adulthood in the initial stages can involve a similar case of mistaken identity.

"I'm working on it . . . being an adult," reports twenty-seven-year-old Debbie, a cosmetics saleswoman. "Sometimes, I feel mature, responsible. Sometimes, I'm in a fog, uncomfortable, depressed."

"I don't feel like an adult," says Barbara, forty-four. "I have a few more goals to accomplish. When my daughter graduates from high school; now that I think about it . . . when both daughters graduate from college, then I can live my life. I can be an adult."

"I was an adult at age six because I could take care of myself," says Alex, fifty-six, a teacher. "But I guess in some ways, I'm really not."

What do these people mean when they speak of adulthood? Is *responsibility* the key word? What about *integrity* or *conformity* or *peace of mind?* The answers aren't simple. For Debbie, Barbara, Alex and millions like them, there is compelling societal pressure to be an adult. "Grow up!" say friends, family and society. "Act your age!" But no one knows exactly what that means.

Susan, a petite twenty-nine-year-old, is married and has one child, Jessica, a bright and inquisitive three-year-old. Susan works part-time to augment the family income, and she has recently returned to the local university to complete her undergraduate studies. One day while fixing breakfast, she hears a television commercial telling her how she can "have it all." Susan grimaces cynically and gives a weary sigh. Lately she has felt like an overtired child. Adult life seems more than she can handle.

Alan, forty-one, an accountant, works for a major automobile company. Recently he has been alternating between "feeling like an imposter" and "just going through the motions." In one poignant therapy session, he confesses tearfully:

> *I don't have the guts to admit that I always wanted to do something more meaningful than count numbers all day for someone else. All day long, all I think about is money. Now I've bought this big house; I've got a huge mortgage and my wife says that I'd better grow up.*

Victoria, sixty-nine, is a mother of ten children and grandmother of seventeen. She has been married to Joe, a retired steel mill worker, for what seems like "all her life." Lately she has been complaining of ill health, but all her tests are negative. Doctors find nothing physically wrong with her. In counseling she speaks quickly but carefully.

"I don't really feel like an adult," she says, her words contrasting with her silver hair and gently wrinkled skin. "I never had the opportunity to grow up. I was too busy trying to raise the kids and trying to do the right thing." Despite her age, Victoria confesses, "I don't even know who I am or what I want. I've spent fifty years married to a man, always doing what he wanted me to do."

The twenty-nine-year-old student, forty-year-old accountant and sixty-nine-year-old grandmother have one thing in common. Despite appearances, none of them feels like an adult. Each has passed the milestones that separate adolescence from adulthood in our society. They can drink, drive, vote and get married. They obey laws and are generally responsible; they conform to what society expects of them. But their behavior does not begin to reflect what they feel. They do not feel able to live up to their own expectations or the expectations of others.

All three are having trouble with traditional adult roles. And they are not the only ones: there are millions like them among us. We can dismiss them all as disturbed and out of sync with our culture — or we can question the validity of traditional roles.

Twenty-five years ago, we Americans were just beginning to understand ourselves psychologically. Today talk shows and play-by-play comments from the "ists" — psychiatrists, psychologists, sociologists and numerous others — have turned us into psychological sophisticates. We routinely delve into once-taboo topics and are rapidly understanding that emotional maturation has little to do with age.

Most clinicians would probably define adulthood according to Freud, as a minimum level of emotional health to be achieved by each individual. In this definition, emotional health means making a reasonable adjustment, reaching a working compromise, with the culture's demands. That assumes the culture is normal. But what if the culture is underdeveloped, ill or evil? Is compromising with or giving into society's demands a valid test of maturity?

One of the pioneers who investigated life stages was Erik Erikson, who relates life tasks to chronological ages. From twenty to sixty, for example, the individual struggles with achieving spousal intimacy and becoming productive or faces isolation and stagnation; at sixty, individuals reflect on their lives and decide whether they have done it "their way" with honesty; if not, they are subject to despair.

Erikson's Adult Development

Adolescence (13-20) — Develops own identity vs. role confusion
Young adult (20-40) — Develops intimacy or becomes isolated
Adulthood (40-60) — Becomes productive or stagnates
Maturity (60+) — Acknowledges pursuit of own desires or despairs

Yale's distinguished social psychologist Daniel Levinson developed a ladder of adult progression that divides life into four sections, each twenty years long, and five age periods of from four to seven years each.

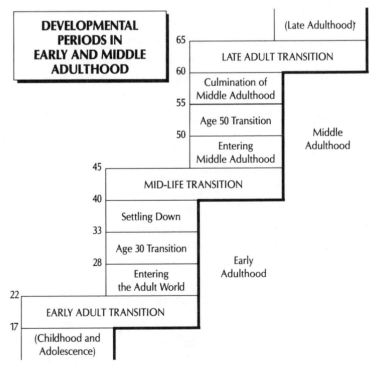

Reprinted by permission of Random House, 1977.

In Levinson's view, the adult world begins between the ages of twenty-two and twenty-eight, when the individual chooses an occupation and enters into a love relationship. At thirty, the individual questions and then begins to modify that initial structure during a transition period. Those who find their initial choices flawed may experience considerable change during this transition and will most likely attempt to complete these changes before settling into a new stage of relative stability. Levinson's ladder continues with alternating age-related periods of equilibrium following each crisis.

Levinson's theory of predictable life crises (a concept popularized by Gail Sheehy's best-selling *Passages*) initiated interest in adulthood processes and made *midlife crisis* a buzzword of the 1970s.

At the same time, a study of Harvard University undergraduates by George Vaillant made some important contributions by re-affirming parts of Erikson's research. In his book *Adaptation To Life*, Vaillant reports that people involved in intimate relationships fare better than those who live alone.

Vaillant also wanted to explore the midlife crisis. Convinced that it was linked to age and common to all cultures, Vaillant continued to observe men from his original sample. He discovered that self-confidence is a key to understanding why some of us experience emotional development while others do not. His research suggests that achieving adulthood is a process of gaining self-confidence and modifying how we defend our personal integrity against the outside world.

On the other coast, psychoanalyst Roger Gould's findings, published in *Transformations*, reported the process of development of 524 white, middle-class respondents. His study followed a series of identity crises that he estimated began in late adolescence and did not culminate until sometime between the ages of thirty-seven and forty-three.

During these crises, the respondents became more independent and adult as they gradually discarded false assumptions. Gould suggests that as we give up our need for security and our illusions of safety, we progress to the next stage.

Gould was venturing close to Jane Loevinger and Robert Kegan's research categorizing ego development. In their conceptualization, progressive levels of ego development are characterized by increasing emotional and cognitive sophistication. These levels progress from simple self-serving, culturally biased thinking based on fears toward more sophisticated, integrated thinking that takes into consideration one's own needs as well as another's and society's at large. While these researchers have done well at pinpointing the minutiae of detail, they make the shift from cultural to emotional awareness seem unnecessarily cumbersome by delineating several "shifts" instead of the emotional/cultural change.

The Jungians don't. It was Swiss psychiatrist Carl Jung who initially focused on the process of individuation, a psychological process of integrating split-off components of the self. For Jungians, self is the essence of existence. To find the self requires an uncomfortable process when one's ego or sense of self breaks away from the emotional, or true self. Eventually, the ego and self are integrated, but not before they:

> *float through ambiguous spaces in the sense of unbounded time through a territory of unclear boundaries and uncertain edges, when it is disidentified from the inner images that have formerly sustained it and have given it a sense of purpose.*

The floating ego is the adulthood crisis. Individuation was believed to be a good thing, although Jungians didn't go so far as to suggest it as mandatory for normal adult development.

Hardliner gerontologists don't agree. "It just doesn't exist!" says Gilbert Brim, director of the Ongoing Project on Midlife for the McArthur Foundation. His team quietly concedes that about 5 percent of the population may "go through something" but cautions that the majority of people who think they are in a midlife crisis are confusing it with a divorce or some other negative life event. Paul Costa and Robert McCrae, two primary adult development researchers at the National Institute of Aging, similarly cannot statistically verify the midlife crisis in their extensive collection of data.

As long as researchers are looking for a time period they will never find the so-called midlife crisis. About 30 percent of those questioned in a recent Gallup poll reported they have had a midlife crisis, and that figure is supported by my clinical observations and those of colleagues looking for the midlife crisis. Those who deny the reality of the adulthood crisis are seldom doctors working in the trenches of clinical settings and so are not called upon to try to understand the emotional development of the person in the crisis. They focus on age — say, the period from forty to forty-five — and consequently miss the clinical forest for the trees.

Emotional Adults: The Real Thing

American novelist Nathaniel Hawthorne once wrote, "No man for any considerable period can wear one face to himself and another to the multitude without finally getting bewildered as to which one may be true." Such bewilderment is the point many of us reach as we begin the transition to true adulthood.

Only when we no longer feel obliged to serve society's demands at the expense of our inner needs can we recapture what our culture has diluted, devalued or deemed unnecessary for outward survival and success. When we make this shift in mindset, we begin to feel authentic emotions, regardless whether they meet the needs of others. We regain the child in us that guides us to what truly matters. At that point, we become ourselves, and we are able to hear our inner voice. As Levinson observes:

> *Internal voices that have been muted for years now clamor to be heard. At times, a vague whispering, the content unclear, but the time indicating grief over lost opportunities, outrage over betrayal by others or guilt over betrayal by oneself. At other times, they come through with a thunderous roar, the content all too clear, stating names and times and places, demanding that something be done to right the balance.*

To understand true adulthood, we must first understand that there are two tracks to be used in defining ourselves: first, as an expression of our culture, and, second, as an expression of emotional needs.

Generally we start life within a safety net of love and security. Our parents are there to teach us the ropes and cushion the blows, to help us survive and succeed in the world. In exchange for their help and support, we work to please our parents, others and the culture at large, while repressing our personal feelings. People who strive to please others or who continue to seek culturally defined experiences are at risk of emotional stagnation.

On the other hand, cable TV tycoon Ted Turner has candidly stated that much of his drive was based on making a dying father proud. Unfortunately, I have counseled many a successful executive who has achieved great wealth and status and now wants an explanation of why he feels so empty.

Cultural Adults: The Great Imposters

By cultural standards, he was an adult. Gray-haired Bill was married, wore three-piece suits and was considered successful. But he was emotionally an impostor. "I was an adult when I was twelve," insists Bill, a stocky seventy-four-year-old security guard.

"How did you know you were an adult?" I inquired.

"Come on. It was different then. I left my father's farm and went out into the world at fifteen. That's the way it was then," he answered. There is no question in Bill's mind that he was an adult by the age of fifteen.

"I was an adult at eighteen," argues Judy, thirty-six, a New York freelance writer.

"How do you know?" I inquired.

"I had adult ideas. Big ideas! You know. And I was responsible, very responsible for my brothers and sisters."

Further inquiry reveals that Bill and Judy have seldom challenged conventional social expectations and neither has experienced the requisite crisis en route to adulthood. Those who accept the prevailing cultural definition of adulthood may never achieve their full sense of being. It stands in the way of their development. Often these people are haunted by the feeling that there must be more to life, but too often they cannot let go of their emotional defenses and respond.

Bob, fifty, an East Coast executive, has his whole life mapped out; he just hasn't found a way to pencil in enjoyment:

> I've had good five-, ten- and twenty-year plans. And I've been lucky enough that they worked out. You have to have backup plans, too. But you're the one who makes it happen. Retirement? Yes. I've organized that. If all goes well, I'll be living down in Florida in my condo by the time I'm sixty. I have a five-year plan for that, too.

There is nothing wrong with careful planning. But it is not sufficient, at least not for Bob. If it were, he would not have found himself in therapy looking to fix the ache within him. He has yet to learn that society's assessment of his success has little or nothing in common with his own inner needs.

As it happened, Bob was caught in the mass layoffs of the 1990s. After the initial upset, he discovered that getting laid off was his "most freeing experience." Now he rides his motorcycle, enjoys his family more and is beginning a new career in consulting.

Take another case, that of Leonard, who runs a chain of retail stores in Florida. "You psychology guys don't know a thing," he taunts. "I'm the head of a business with more than 1,000 employees. I could buy and sell you." But Leonard, who has spent his sixty-four years mastering the techniques of economic survival and prosperity, has entered psychotherapy with the complaint that all his accomplishments do not seem to be satisfying. As with Bob — something is missing.

These people may not be as adult as they think they are, but they have taken an important first step. They have made it in the world. They have demonstrated their financial and personal independence, separating from their parents, creating new allegiances and assuming some responsibility to the larger community.

In fact, we cannot become true adults unless we have become adults in our social milieu. Take the example of Lynn, forty-one, who comes from a small town in Maine. Lynn married at twenty-one and immediately started a family. Her domineering husband made sure that Lynn remained financially dependent. As a result, Lynn may never attain true adulthood, even though she is emotionally ready. She is too frightened of the unknown and too convinced that she is unable to take care of herself:

> *I've had this crisis thing you keep talking about. I mean, I'm still going through it right now. But I guess I am still afraid of getting out in the world. It's really scary out there. The other day I was reading about a woman getting attacked in Portland in a parking lot in broad daylight. And*

since I've just learned to drive this past year, I've been even more cautious than usual. I guess I'm a little different than most girls my age; I mean just driving for less than a year. Doug never pushed me, and the kids' school was three blocks down. You asked me if I am an adult; well, I'd have to say that in some ways I am, in other ways I'm not.

True adulthood for Lynn could easily happen if she would just use the energies that she has been expending on others to increase her autonomy. Learning to drive at forty was an important first step. Earning a living would be the one that finally ended her emotional reign of terror.

Women like Lynn squander their inner strength on caretaking, frequently tolerating abuse to keep the peace and maintain the family. Their husbands waste their energies on acting like bosses. In reality they are as childish as their wives — dependent, in fact, on their caretaking spouses to help them meet the demands of daily living. These irresponsible men are as far from adulthood as their dependent women.

Three Ingredients Of Emotional Adulthood

I will not make a case for autonomy and responsibility as components of adulthood, since these traits often create the cultural definitions of adulthood and have only a moderating effect on internal concerns and emotional needs. Besides, most people are inundated with responsibilities and fear of dependency. When people enter my office tired and empty, they are always responsible and seemingly autonomous. But the degree of emotional neglect of themselves is astounding, and their defenses against experiencing their true needs and feelings provide a cultural wall around them. The problem is how to create a shift in their defensive structure.

War Of The Grown-Ups:
Comparison Of False With True Adults

Cultural Adults (False maturation)	Emotional Adults (True maturation)
Prevalence: 70 percent	30 percent
Mode of operating: Intellectual	Emotional
Themes: Status, convention, money	Awareness; respect for feelings, needs
Relationships: Role-based	Emotionally responsive
Play: Competitive	Noncompetitive
Values/Politics: Conservative	Liberal
Motivating emotions: Fear	Curiosity
Secondary emotions: Anger	Depression
Orientation: Closed, cautious	Open, experimental, spontaneous
Experience: Culturally confirmed	Emotionally confirmed
Social relations: Superficial	Emotionally deep
Language: Power, status, security	Needs, feelings
Charity: "Right thing to do"	Empathy/kindness
Enemy: Others	Emotional inauthenticity
Goals: Culturally defined success	Personally meaningful living
Relation to self: Lies, half-truths	Authenticity
Relation to others: Stereotyped versions	Emotional attributions

We know that certain external experiences may trigger the onset of emotional adulthood. Subsequently, an "ignition" of the proper internal ingredients may create the "combustion" necessary for the shift to adulthood. The ingredients are recognition of your vulnerability, respect for your emotional life and reintegration of your spiritual side.

Vulnerability

The first step toward adulthood is the realization that no matter how hard you try, you don't fit and never will. The trick is not to try to fit the cultural standards of success. The trick is to be yourself.

Most people are loath to view themselves as vulnerable. And that is not surprising, since, as a culture, we clearly undervalue the trait of vulnerability. But accepting your vulnerability is the first step necessary for adult readiness. You have to acknowledge your life struggles and, in effect, wear them on your sleeve. You make yourself accessible — and people connect with you.

Undoubtedly, more conservative members of our society, such as right-wing talk show host Rush Limbaugh and his followers, would not agree. They view vulnerability as undesirable, even un-American, and feel that we are in danger of becoming a nation of victims.

Yet, accepting vulnerability is the only road to emotional adulthood. You have to ask yourself whether you are enough of a person to stand up to our prevailing culture of emotional intolerance.

"I don't like to be vulnerable," says Art, a sixty-five-year-old retired schoolteacher. "How in the hell can I tell that the other guy won't take advantage of it?" Art had little to worry about regarding other men. His wife of seven years left him. She was tired of this tough guy and his intolerance of her problems.

"Sure I can talk about what I'm afraid of," reports Art. "I just didn't know anyone would listen or was interested." He later admits, "I'm scared that I'll push everyone away and eventually die alone and empty." Not a bad fear to acknowledge for starters. What are the other ones? More honesty and courage in talking about his life struggles would have made Art more accessible to himself and to the wife who abandoned him.

"I don't know where to begin to look for my vulnerabilities," says John, a sixty-two-year-old from Durham, North Carolina — and it's not unusual for my clients to make this comment, since most people have learned to hide their vulnerability early in life. You can begin by re-owning your major disappointments and pain. Parenthetically, most people defend themselves vigorously against the Big Three primary emotions of sadness, anger and fear.

Respect For Emotions

Perhaps the most difficult part with the move to emotional adulthood is leaving a lifelong pattern of following societal rules of cultural success and accepting an experiential world of honest feelings. To live by one's feelings, to live what philosopher Sam Keen — author of *Fire in the Belly* — and others have called the passionate life, may be the greatest challenge an individual faces. It is incredibly frightening to leave something for what seems at first an abstract ideal, and it requires courage to make the commitment to oneself. Perhaps this is the reason most people will never become emotional adults.

After one accepts vulnerability and can address one's emotional struggles, a newfound respect for the internal life emerges. There is an increased awareness, and a person begins to live — spontaneously and reactively!

Let's return to a remorseful Art:

> *You know now I understand what a prick I had been to my wife. I didn't realize how I came off. I didn't mean to hurt her and wasn't aware that I did. I mean, who the hell do I think I am anyway? It's weird this realization, this awareness.*

Whether you like it or not, you are governed by your emotional life. Why not start living it instead of fighting it?

Reintegrating The Spiritual

The final phase of achieving true adulthood involves reintegrating the underdeveloped sides of one's personality. Psychologist Wayne Dyer has a wonderful saying he uses in his lectures: "You are not a human being having a spiritual experience: you are a spiritual being having a human experience." Perhaps the saying has been overused recently, but I suggest you surrender to its simple truth.

Gerontologists Paul Costa and Robert McCrae of the National Institute on Aging have pinpointed "openness to experience" as a lifelong trait that makes for successful aging. I think it is an attitude that can be nurtured and developed. Most of us were born with it, but somewhere in our childhood we began to lose it. When we can recapture that lost open child within us, a new awareness emerges.

Dave, a forty-five-year-old General Motors vice president, is a good example of openness emerging. Asked for his view of adulthood, Dave hit the standard buttons of the cultural definition: "It's to get ahead in life. You know, marriage and family. Raising them and later, you know, I guess retiring down to Arizona. Making something of yourself."

I asked him what he was making of his life — reminding him that his wife and coworkers had sent him into treatment for being too critical, serious and emotionally distant. "A mess!" he retorted quickly, then paused to think. Dave knew he was so serious and driven and critical because he thought being an adult meant "getting the job done right." That's a good company attitude, but even at the company people couldn't live with his overdeveloped drive. Dave finally admitted:

> You know, I don't even like myself like this. It's not my nature. I used to have fun, laugh, have a personality. But it's been gone for over twenty years. I don't have any real

friends. You know, I was so good at telling everyone else what to do, I never really did anything for myself.

Eventually Dave and I worked on reintegrating a delightful mischievous part of himself. He now plays office pranks on employees, and they play pranks on him. This signals the beginning of his shift into emotional adulthood.

Spiritual reintegration does not mean divorcing ourselves from the values of our childhood religions — though that may happen. It means connecting with the spirited part of ourselves, that lighthearted part that can turn almost any event into a joyful experience.

4

Metamorphosis: Shift, Storm And Homeward Bound

---

*The whole of the individual
is nothing but the process of giving birth
to himself; indeed we should be fully
born when we die although it is
the tragic fate of most individuals to
die before they are born.*

— Erich Fromm,
The Sane Society

I deally, the shift from a cultural to a personal framework of meaning occurs spontaneously in the process of achieving true adulthood. Society's needs and sociocultural values shift into the background. Emotional and personal needs shift into the foreground. We experience real perceptual changes.

Let's use the elderly as an example. Youth initially views elderly persons as a different genus or species. When we become emotionally adult, elderly persons are finally seen as the same species with salient age characteristics such as gray hair and wrinkles.

Remember the day you saw your parents as old? Or the day you saw people five years older than you as just your age? I remember how womanly airline stewardesses seemed when I was in my early twenties, and how girlish they seemed by the time I had reached my thirties. Columnist Richard Cohen had a similar realization.

The cops of my youth always seemed to be big, even huge and, of course, they were older than I was. Then one day, they were neither. In fact, some of them were kids, short kids at that. The day comes when you realize that all the football players in the game you're watching are younger than you. Instead of being big men, they were merely big kids.

Countdown To Adulthood

How long does the transition to adulthood take? Most people who have made it are uncertain. It's hard to judge since the awareness of the process is generally not felt until it is well under way. Consequently, the exact onset of true adulthood is difficult to pinpoint. In a preliminary study, I found a range of "adulthood crises" lasting from eighteen to sixty months. On the average they lasted about two-and-a-half years. It seems to take a long time for adults to grow up.

Revolution Or Evolution?

Does everybody have to have a crisis to become a true adult? The answer, I believe, is a resounding *yes*. Like a book of truths that we choose to open, some of us read quickly, while others savor each word. On the other hand, most decide not to even pick the book up in the first place. Bold people, emotionally reactive people and those who have held back much in anger seem to experience a revolution in the adulthood crisis, making loud noises concerning themselves and those around them. More cautious people unfold in a quieter, evolutionary way.

Divorcing One's Parents

As we begin to move toward what we find personally relevant, we move away from the first culture we ever experienced, the family in which we grew up struggling for autonomy.

Struggles are often a two-way street. "My children won't talk to me," laments a meddling sixty-two-year-old mother. I then explain that her children need less advice and more friendship.

"My mother's driving me crazy," reports the forty-two-year-old burgeoning adult daughter.

Blaming parents is necessary to a point; it is fundamental to a separation and subsequent understanding of a healthy family system. Past a certain point, blaming parents blocks emotional adulthood processes.

There is a memorable scene in the film *Postcards From The Edge* in which the director, played by Gene Hackman, gives advice to an actor (Meryl Streep) on the adulthood crisis and her relationship with her mother. "At some point, you just stop and say 'fuck it. I start with me.' "

The metamorphosis into true adulthood begins with disillusionment in our dream about the way adult life is supposed to be. The experience is eye-opening and depressing, and yet, if we stay open to the process, it will be incredibly rewarding.

The feeling of uneasiness that accompanies the process seems to come from nowhere and be linked to nothing. "I've never been this vulnerable in my life!" reports Kerry, a thirty-two-year-old banking executive. "And, I'm not sure I can do it," she adds tearfully. At the same time she reports that she feels miserable and disconnected from all the people around her and cannot continue the way things are.

"I couldn't take it one more day," says Carl, a fifty-two-year-old ophthalmologist. "Everything was all screwed up. I thought I was going crazy."

Perhaps it seems a little crazy, but it's normal crazy. Welcome to adulthood!

Triggering Events

Any number of life's events may trigger an adulthood crisis by making the individual more vulnerable and yet more open to change and more receptive to inner feelings. But the crisis isn't the event: it's the individual's reaction to it. Some will shake off dramatic events in their lives and continue as before; others will collapse. And still others will turn into true adults.

There can be a variety of potential triggers, from the death of a parent, spouse, child or friend to a life-threatening illness, accident or trauma. A career change, the loss of a job, a divorce or a separation can also light the fuse. But while these kinds of important life events trigger the transition in some people, they *haven't* happened to most people who describe the metamorphosis into adulthood.

In the Academy Award-winning film *Moonstruck*, Olympia Dukakis portrayed a wise woman who searched for reasons why her middle-aged husband was having an affair. She concluded: "Cosmo, I just want you to know that no matter what you do, you're gonna die just like everybody else!"

Death

For Elizabeth, 47, a San Francisco homemaker and former nurse, the death of both of her parents within two months triggered a crisis:

I became very aware of my own mortality. In my mind, parents are not supposed to die — especially my mother. She was a powerhouse of emotion, and somehow the thought of this very vital woman dying put me in touch with the fact that I will die, too. The knowledge that life will end someday has also made a great impression in altering my values. If all ends in the abyss, then why should material things take on the significance they do? Why get involved in petty minutiae if it will eventually become meaningless? Life seems to be a concentrated effort at denying death — at cloaking this unknown terror in material costume.

Elizabeth continues:

I truly felt like an orphan. As long as my parents were alive, I could always go home. Even though they were aging and ill, somehow they represented a safe haven in the midst of uncertainty. The first image that surfaced immediately after their deaths was a picture of myself wearing ice skates and being pushed into the center of an ice rink at high speed. My legs were shaky and I didn't know where I would land. The rink was deserted; I was all alone skating at high velocity into nowhere. You know, I think it was at this point that the child in me grew up and I internalized the fact that I was indeed capable of functioning very adequately by myself. One day, soon after my mother's sudden death, I went to the house and opened the small bedroom closet she always kept locked. I envisioned all sorts of treasures lying behind that door. But when I entered, I saw things that I had bought for her years ago. This necklace of hers, some old but beautiful clothes — a dress that she had worn to my wedding, an inexpensive lipstick that I had given her for a birthday. And then I realized that the treasures were in the meanings that were attached to the objects and not their monetary worth. I just stood there and cried!

Writer Joan Gould recognizes that her transition was occasioned by her widowhood. In a *New York Times Magazine* article, she says:

Looking back, I see the period between college and marriage as a time when I learned I was alone, committed to a self that I didn't encounter again until my second adolescence during the early sessions of widowhood.

Many individuals are suddenly forced to grow up when they find themselves on their own, often for the first time, after a divorce or the death of a spouse. "I got married so young. Now, I want to get out and see who I am and do what everybody else did before they got married and had children," says Mary Lynn, forty-nine, after her divorce.

Trauma

Physical trauma potentially provides another trigger. I know of a man who, during a swimming accident, had a profound near-death experience that he is convinced changed his life. I am not certain whether the experience changed his life or provided him with a reason to live his life the way he wanted to. A similar change sometimes occurs in middle-aged men and women after a heart attack. As Michael, a sensitive, shell-shocked, forty-two-year-old teacher, reports:

> *I feel that I have a second chance! I just never thought about my life much. Took it for granted; smoking, no exercise. Now I'm a health nut. And I realize that I really haven't been doing what I wanted with my life. Now I want to make some changes — this time for me instead of others.*

Her husband's abuse triggered the adulthood process for Joyce, forty-four, a factory worker in Detroit who came from a small Tennessee town:

> *I was married quite young — child bride and all. But in the South in that time people did that sort of thing — you know, married young. Anyway, before I knew it, I had babies and all. My husband was abusive by today's standards, and he'd get me good with the "switch." But I didn't know it at the time. I thought that it was the price you had to pay for marriage. I had no choice, given my two babies at the time. I had to grow up.*

Birth

Childbirth can trigger the transition process. Birthing can shift the defenses and increase vulnerability, as it did with Judy Goldsmith, former president of the National Organization for Women (NOW). In a magazine article, Goldsmith tells how the birth of her first child launched her into adulthood:

> *I had two very specific reactions when the nurse first put Rachel in my arms. One was absolute desperation and apprehension. Now, in this moment of truth, there was no doubt in my mind that motherhood was not instinctive! I was a novice, a beginner, no two ways about it. Fortunately,*

so was Rachel. The other reaction was awe at the sheer wonder of this little creature. I believed the medical experts who said that a newborn's eyes can't focus, but it seemed that she looked at me with a wisdom and seriousness that underscored the responsibilities that lay ahead. She was heart-stopping in her beauty, touching in her vulnerability and splendid in her health and strength.

Birthdays, retirements and other poignant life events offer additional potential triggers. They make us pause, if only for a few moments, and consider the direction of our lives. For example, French artist Henri Rousseau's awakening occurred when he retired as a customs officer at forty-one and picked up a paintbrush. Japanese painter Katsushika Hokusai similarly claimed, "I was born at the age of fifty," and similarly began his life's work.

Not all birthdays are equally thought provoking. Why some are and some aren't is not clear, but it probably has to do with how closely the individual's life meets his or her expectations. In our society, thirty, forty and fifty seem to be significant milestones.

Men often use these timeposts to measure their financial and career success, while women tend to evaluate their physical appearance and the welfare of their families.

Gerontologist Susan Krauss Whitbourne of the University of Massachusetts at Amherst has found that birthdays hold more meaning for women than for men.

Why one birthday hits harder than another may have more to do with how we use these dates as a measure of our life expectations. Paris, homemaker, age thirty-three, speaks of her recent marking:

I have no idea why thirty-three is so hard. You would have thought thirty was the difficult one, eh? I guess it is hitting me hard because so much is up in the air. I mean, my relationship is uncertain, my money situation is unstable, my kids are driving me crazy. And I'm fighting with my mother and sisters. I mean, they don't respect me and I'm not going to take it anymore. Anyway, thirty-three — you'd think life would be great, but I'm spending it mostly depressed. I wouldn't do thirty-three again!

The Seven-Year Itch

For those who marry in their mid-twenties an adulthood crisis is frequently the catalyst for an office affair in their thirties. What makes these affairs so devastating is that usually only one of the partners is going through the crisis at any given time; so disruption and blame are virtually unavoidable.

According to the Census, the median age for divorce in the United States is 32.5 years for woman and 34.9 for men. This is also the peak period for outpatient psychotherapy, and the statistical bulge here is almost double both earlier and later rates. But the interesting thing is that the patients are not going into therapy to deal with their divorce.

Who Enters Therapy?			
%			
50			
40		X	
30		X	
20	X	X	X
10	X	X	X
	(21-30)	(31-40)	(41-50)

Courtesy of Ken Howard, Ph.D., Northwestern University Psychology Dept.

Large epidemiological studies at the National Institute of Mental Health and Northwestern University have found that the most common diagnoses for outpatient therapy are "adjustment disorder" and "depression," which show signs and symptoms identical to those of the adult crisis.

My own observation is that since the average age of adult crisis occurs in one's early thirties, therapy use and divorce rates are all linked. It is also telling that affairs are most likely to occur in this early thirties age group.

Altered States

Michael Blumenthal's trigger lies at some distance from the norm. Blumenthal, a middle-aged university professor, found his adulthood through a recent LSD experience and published an account of it:

> In my early and mid-twenties, LSD and other psychedelics changed me, in ways both subtle and palpable. Whatever measure I have had since then of detachment and equanimity — whatever sense that the world of our daily stresses and significances is but a small shadow of a world of both greater power and significance — I owe, at least in part, to those not so much visionary as envisioned states, states I have also felt access to during periods of poetic inspirations, when I felt as though I were taking dictation directly from somewhere "beyond" the ordinary. Yet in more mature adulthood, there are actions that such experiences as I have attempted to describe here could — perhaps ought to — lead toward. One might easily be inspired to become a more active environmentalist, to do volunteer work for people with AIDS, to live more closely with nature, to adopt homeless children, to name but a few of the possibilities. One might simply find oneself more capable of love and forgiveness, of generosity of spirit. In other words, it has provided me with a greater commitment to this world . . . and a greater detachment from it. And — strange though it may seem to say so — I am convinced that it has helped me to become a better, more loving father. For it has helped me to see my son as no longer entirely my son, but life's son, and my life as no longer entirely my life, but part of a greater continuum and force.

Instant karma prospects notwithstanding, no LSD trip can trigger true emotional adulthood. More often drugs or alcohol delay the development of emotional adulthood. Singer Bonnie Raitt's recovery experiences are a case in point.

During semester breaks from college Raitt began earning money by playing the blues in clubs and cafés. She gained a reputation for her smoky, soulful singing voice, as well as for her mastery of the slide guitar.

Although she built a loyal audience, her popularity was limited. Frustrated, she turned to alcohol and drugs. Soon she had also built a reputation for herself as a hard-drinking blues woman. Many times she'd stay up all night drinking tequila.

"There was a romance about drinking and doing blues," she said in a recent interview. "These blues guys had been professional drinkers for years, and I wanted to prove that I could hold my liquor with them."

In 1983, she began to slide, and Warner Brothers dropped her. A love affair of four years ended, and Raitt sank deeper and deeper into alcohol and cocaine. Recovery began in 1987 when Raitt started putting her life back together with help from an alcohol recovery group. Sober, she had no trouble taking the Grammy for Best Album two years later, and she married happily. For Bonnie Raitt recovery and achieving true adulthood went hand in hand.

Coming Out

Homosexual adulthood, while really not different from heterosexual adulthood, may be accelerated or delayed because of the coming-out process. Ed, a handsome blond, blue-eyed, thirty-five-year-old Toronto clothing representative suggests a new coming out that has little to do with his coming into his own:

I don't know really when adulthood is for me. I still don't feel like an adult. I mean, I'm about eighteen years old inside, and I'm not certain if that is really good or bad. Just the way it is. I came out when I was twenty, and my family was totally accepting. So in that sense, it wasn't really anything to do with feeling like an adult inside. But I know people who have come out and began to feel adult at the same time. And I think with more and more kids coming out younger and younger — age twelve and thirteen, it is changing. I mean the days when the quiet bachelor brother reveals his true self on his thirtieth birthday, and the family goes into some sort of crisis — I mean, those days are over, for sure. No, I still don't feel like an adult, and I certainly don't know when it begins. Does anyone?

Career

Actor John Rubenstein, son of legendary pianist Arthur Rubenstein, addresses his difficult transition: "I was the baby of the family, extremely adaptable, treated as a junior adult." Today his own man, he once withered in the shadow of his father. Rubenstein came out of his family with "an underdeveloped muscle of self-esteem. The music of me — exactly who I was — got lost. I was a lightbulb, and Dad was the spotlight." After a 1980 Tony for his role in the play about the deaf, *Children Of A Lesser God*, Rubenstein observed a change in himself:

Yes, I had a very slow, gradual realization that I had made myself secondary to conform to Dad's life. Parts of me were put on hold, parts that needed to breathe. Instead of driving and pushing, I slowly discovered in myself an ability to stand and enjoy. It's a personal refocusing that goes beyond a midlife crisis. Now I'm happier, more interested in things in the world, less selfish. I could always be the son of Arthur Rubenstein when he was alive, but I can't hide behind that anymore.

Inner Triggers

Since the shift to adulthood is essentially a psychological process, and not a social one, there is often no observable trigger. Indeed, most people report just a general feeling of disillusionment that seems to disrupt the emotional system's delicate defensive balance.

"For me, this happened a couple of years ago," reports folk-rock star Kenny Loggins, forty-five:

> *It wasn't so much a conscious decision as just something that came over me as a precursor to a re-evaluation of my business and eventually my marriage. This wasn't temporary insanity, with everything going out the window. In my mid-life clarity, it became easier for me to see and feel what was and wasn't working, and I simply kept the things that were!*

On The Road: Disillusionment, Questioning, Awakening

There's a wonderful Hallmark card showing a cartoon character lying in bed looking forlorn. Its caption reads: "Rude awakening #457: Nobody really cares what your GPA was." And so begins the disillusionment phase — and end of a dream about the way life was supposed to be and the beginning of the way adult life really is.

Our earliest life strategies are modeled on cultural ideals. The ideals are important and, to a degree, we need them to show us how to survive and succeed in the culture. They constitute what Daniel Levinson calls the adult dream — an ideal of the way adult life is supposed to be. And we go about the business of trying to make the dream happen as if we have busted out of Leavenworth prison. Naturally, we get hurt as we find out that the world isn't here merely to fulfill our fantasies. Sometimes we adjust ourselves and try harder, but eventually we adjust the dream, since most dreams are constructed in adolescence and haven't been tested out in the real world.

When these cultural ideals conflict with our own internal sense of being, however, we rarely battle for our inside world. Instead we remake ourselves to match society's expectations and images — and that's when the trouble begins.

Most of us form an image of adulthood based on these ideals somewhere in our late teens. Unless we renovate and upgrade the image — our dream of the way adult life is supposed to be — we are doomed to failure.

Dissipating The Mirage

"An era can be said to end when its basic illusions end," wrote playwright Arthur Miller — and much of emotional adulthood has to do with giving up the old illusions in favor of dreams that are more consistent with our inner selves. Whether our newly adjusted dreams are realistic or not becomes the domain of the psychotherapist. But when they are inconsistent with who we are — that becomes the domain of our souls.

"It's a blow to our narcissism," says Northwestern University gerontologist David Gutmann, speaking of the adult dream disillusionment. "Nobody likes it," and we quietly mourn as we come to terms with the idea that we may not be "discovered" or make the football team or become the president of the company. We come to realize that cultural achievements may not be essential for personal happiness. As true adults, we tolerate disappointment, separation and frailties in ourselves and others. We understand that these are necessary and fundamental parts of adult life. We who can cope, who can maintain realistic goals in the face of challenging circumstances, are able to nurture ourselves and others.

"Those of you who do not have your life planned out, don't worry. It wouldn't turn out the way you planned it in any event," said Vince Foster, whose haunting words delivered to Arkansas Law School graduates foreshadowed his unexpected suicide in 1993 in a Washington, D.C. park. Foster was a key government aide and Bill and Hillary Clinton's personal attorney. On the outside, it appeared that he had it all. But the inside probably told a different story.

Questions, Questions, Questions

Often we are obsessed with questions: Do I like my work? Why did I get married? Do I want to stay married? Why don't I have children? Why do I have so many children? Why am I not happier? Who am I?

Janice, thirty-eight, a legal secretary and single parent to a sixteen-year-old asks, "Should I have a baby? Is that what's missing?"

Jane, a forty-year-old suburban homemaker states, "I search every face for an answer. I try to draw strength from family and friends, but I can't. I have been sucked dry, and they have nothing left to give."

In true adulthood an individual may realize that he does not need to be chairman of the board to be happy. Another may have pop singer Peggy Lee's deep sense of disillusionment. "Is this all there is?" we ask constantly.

We pay a price for disillusionment and questioning, and the price is deeply emotional. Our dominant moods fluctuate between two primary feeling states: depression stemming from dissolving of the dream and anxiety stemming from fear of the new.

Depression has to do with mourning the former life and is focused on role and identity, meaning and purpose. Anxiety has to do with anticipating the new adult and manifests itself in constant worrying (e.g., concerns for financial survival, what the neighbors will think).

We commonly fluctuate between the two states, for adults-in-transition shed their old skins by questioning everything about themselves and others as they awaken for the first time.

Awakening

Once the shift to contacting deep emotions begins, our perception changes. We see things more clearly, awakening to what is real. During this state of psychological awareness, the meaning of life becomes more than a preoccupation. It becomes almost an obsession. We can understand the adult perspective in the film *Butterflies are Free:* "Ha! I'd rather be blind," Eddie Albert retorts as he confronts Goldie Hawn's immature and emotionally blind character.

As we awaken, we question who we are and what we are doing; we haven't any answers. Emotionally, we feel as if we are in a thick fog. We can barely see our feet below, and we have no clear idea of where we are or where we are going. At each step we could encounter terra firma or quicksand. There is only one way out. Zombie-like, we continue, haunted by the fear of staying where we are and yet fearful of being strangers in a strange land.

Three Phases of Emotional Adulthood

We pass through three phases in the process of developing emotional adulthood — destruction, creation and preservation. And these phases involve more than just wrestling with values. This passage is more than experimentation with new ideas — it is emotional life or death!

Stage One: Destruction

Most non-Western cultures recognize death as an entry into the next phase of existence, an integral part of the natural order; our society has yet to recognize death's necessity. In the destruction stage of our development, however, we are ready to bury those parts of ourselves that have become obsolete. In burying our former selves we shift emphasis. We relegate those who have helped us survive, culturally, to the background. Others, who fit into our new scheme, become more central. We move from being culturally or other-directed to being inner-directed, personal, self-directed. We have a sense of what matters and is meaningful.

Los Angeles clinical social worker Joel Sekely describes the state of turmoil between the meaningful and cultural aspects of self as the process of trying on a suit of clothes. We listen to the salesperson telling us the suit is a fine fit. But we know there is something wrong: it feels too snug in the shoulders, waist or hips. But when we look in the mirror we are amazed that from an outsider's perspective the suit appears to fit. Nothing has changed outwardly.

In the destructive stage we give up our former way of life, letting go of the routine and the familiar. We see more clearly what we have done in the past, as did Greg, age thirty-seven:

> *I realized I had been just using women. I never really gave a shit about their feelings. I didn't even know that women had feelings. I didn't know they were people. Now that I think about it, I guess I'm talking about me. I didn't know that I had feelings and that I was real. Now I realize what I had done in my late twenties and the tons of women that I probably had hurt. If they're listening, I'm sorry, I didn't know what I was doing.*

Sometimes we become anxious, fearful, disconnected and even depressed. To sustain us there is only the tentative vision that life will be better later, as an adult. As Jane, a thirty-seven-year-old homemaker describes it:

> *The idea of a tomorrow looms as an impossible dream. Like Don Quixote jousting at windmills, I, too, joust at the reality of a better tomorrow. So consumed am I with today that I think I can no longer believe in the existence of a*

tomorrow. I can no longer do — let alone repeat — the most minor of family and wifely duties.

People describe this detachment as a hovering above life without being able to touch down. Others compare it to a thick fog that limits visibility so that they can barely see their own feet. Whatever the metaphor, the feeling is clearly one of isolation, of being cut off from others.

Says Jane:

I have never been so alone. The cold of this wilderness is translated into bodily cold. I can never be warm again. The warmth of self contentment and well-being is alien to me. How can anything survive on this Arctic tundra? I can think only of survival from minute to minute.

At forty-eight, Harvard philosopher George Santayana walked out of the classroom in the middle of a lecture. Jan Williams, also forty-eight, had a similar experience. A nurse and teacher, she said one day, "I've done enough prim and proper. Now I just want to hit the road and travel to exotic places." Jan was lucky. A legacy from her father gave her the chance to pursue her dream. She has visited Hawaii, the Galapagos Islands and Patagonia in her travels and keeps exploring.

When we enter this destruction phase of our transition to adulthood, we sometimes cannot let go of the past, as in Stephen's case. "Accounting is so boring," he says. "I'm seriously considering being a tour guide at a museum. You know it's just crazy enough that I might do it!" In pursuit of his dream, Stephen did quit accounting. He found a job as a tour guide, but his earnings could not compare to his previous salary. Stephen had a difficult time defending his new position to his wife. The arrival of a new baby further weakened his position. Stephen returned to accounting, but he is not happy.

Often a person feels stripped and bereft, as if something has been taken and nothing is replacing it. The fear is that there is no self, no defined voice to emerge. A typical psychotherapy patient explains the fear this way:

> *I see myself now as a bunch of illusions, with no center . . . or as this big black hole. Now that we are getting nearer to me, I get more concerned. Perhaps there isn't a me. It's just a hole. And what people would want to get close to me? Perhaps I'm just an illusion and there really isn't anything underneath.*

But there is something underneath, a whole person. The fog lifts as mysteriously as it came. And one day we realize that we have given birth — to ourselves.

Stage Two: Creation

"I just had a baby and it's me!" remarks thirty-nine-year-old engineer Phil. "I don't feel the turmoil anymore," gleefully exclaims Donna, thirty-seven. "Don't get me wrong, I still have problems. But I don't have all the anxiety I had before."

As newly formed adults, we are less naïve and more sure of ourselves, less fearful and more clearheaded. "I no longer need my husband the same way," says Jamie, forty-two, in her newly discovered emotional strength. "I can take care of myself."

There is a subtle shift in cognition and a new attitude toward what can be changed and what can't. We are able to accept the things we cannot change, we are able to live with life's ambiguities. "You grow up the first day you really have a good laugh at yourself," said actress Ethel Barrymore.

We experience a change in thinking; time is liquid. We recognize that there are no black-and-white answers, but rather a multitude of colors. We know that life is serious, but we allow room for play. We discover our inner voice, and it, too, becomes more reflective of the ups and downs of living — the voice of the adult that is here to stay.

Getting Our Voices Back

Often we have kept silent, subject to the whims and demands of others. Silence is the ultimate accommodation because the silent individual lives by the rules and is on the receiving end of power. As Roger Gould describes it, the individual blindly follows parental precepts in the belief that this will ensure safety. But, in fact, silence is an extremely unhealthy position, as Sandy's case demonstrates.

Sandy came from a traditional working class family. She learned quickly that obedience to a father was all important. Pregnant at eighteen, married at nineteen, soon a mother of three, she ignored an unfulfilling marriage by shopping or by doting on her children's achievements. Convinced of her voicelessness, Sandy believed that killing herself would mean little, since there was very little about her that mattered. She seriously entertained thoughts of throwing herself into the Detroit River.

She decided instead on therapy. For several sessions, Sandy was unable to look me in the eye. She could not afford the risk of eye contact, she later explained, because I had the power to "put ideas" into her head. I also had the power to make her admit things to herself that "could not be true."

After several prolonged sessions of silence, she admitted she longer loved her husband. "When I was seventeen and about to get married," she said, "all I thought about was whether my husband was a good provider. That's all I really cared about — you know, security. Because that's what my parents told me I should care about."

Unprepared for adulthood, one incident soon became a focal point in her metamorphosis. "I had the most horrendous experience," Sandy sobbed one day:

I never parked next to a parking meter before, and I didn't know what to do. So I waited and I waited and I waited until I saw somebody else put money in. And then I panicked when I thought I may not have the right change. I'm so embarrassed. I'm sure my nine-year-old could have done it.

Eventually Sandy's new self emerged, defined by genuine needs and authentic feelings in the form of her own voice. Although she criticized herself for not knowing how to put money in the parking meter, she found a way around her dilemma. By observing others, she discovered how to succeed in this particular situation, and her discovery had implications for the future. Sandy understood that it didn't matter whether she was faster or slower or more or less skillful than others. What mattered was that she could rely on herself to find her way. As Sandy says, "There's part of me that didn't realize how important my intuition is — that it guides me and I can listen to it."

Brent, a thirty-one-year-old auto designer, recounts a similar experience when he re-examined his adult models:

It was only last year when I realized that things at work weren't so black-and-white. I went into the field thinking, "Well, someday I'll be supervisor or move into this section." But now I know I wouldn't want to be like most of the people who I meet in positions of authority. They're workaholics and have no personal life. I learned there's a price to pay for all that success. You know, I probably make half of what they do, maybe a third of some of them, and I don't think they are any happier. In fact, I know they're not.

Ernest Becker believes we defensively pursue careers and cultural tasks in order to deny death. Yet that does not explain why people fight death because they have a mission to complete or a project to continue. As did the concert pianist who practiced on keys drawn on the walls of the Auschwitz death camp, we secretly practice the real ambitions that are more an affirmation of our inner lives.

Bryan, a forty-year-old attorney, explains his experience:

I know it strikes most people as bizzare, but when I gave up a law practice to work on a farm, people thought I had a mental breakdown or something. For the first time in my life I'd come to my senses, if you ask me. Yeah, the money's not the same, but I don't care; I can sleep at night.

Our struggles mirror the human condition. An old self is dead; a new one has been created. It is no wonder that death and rebirth themes so often figure prominently in our dreams. "In my dream," says Debbie, twenty-six, "I go back to my father's grave and tell him that I am changing. I want to see if he accepts the new me. I have so many questions I want to ask, but even in the dream I know I can't."

Susan, thirty-four, describes her adult encounter with her dead mother:

I enter my parents' bedroom, and they're both dead. The bed is covered with a floral bedspread, and my mother is lying upside down with her feet where the pillows are. She soothes me and strokes my hair saying, "I'm with your father now . . . it's okay. I want you to go on and do what you have to do." I am scared because she looks terrible, but she reassures me and I begin to get a really strong feeling.

Elizabeth, a thirty-two-year-old writer, reveals another dimension of her creation by dreaming of a significant person who acts as an inspiration for her adult self:

My parents' cleaning lady used to do things special for each of us girls, and I never felt she was gone, though she died almost ten years ago. I had this dream where I talked to my mother and sister. In the dream Sarina [the maid] was sophisticated with a 1940s hat, and she said, "Hello

Elizabeth." And I said, "What's with all this Elizabeth for-
mality — it's me . . . Bizzy." I wanted her to treat me as a
little girl, not as an adult. I was sad. I mean I think I lost her
and let her down. I wanted to make her proud and act like
the sophisticated adult she wanted. I was doubting myself
lately and having difficulty getting motivated, and she came
by and gave me the kick in the pants I needed.

"We have landed — the Eagle has landed" blares our
personal Mission Control. We have selves, and this time
they are worth fighting for.

Stage 3: Preservation

"Each new landscape, now you know, is a stepping
stone, till you're safe at home," sings jazz-pop vocalist
Michael Franks. And at this stage, things do not look
quite the same; our vision is somehow clearer.

Mark Gerzon, thirty-eight, acknowledged his own
awakening in *Coming Into Our Own:*

On one hand was the pain, which I had been blocking
out and denying for years. On the other hand was joy, a
deep serenity and profound aliveness that I did not know
existed. The first half of my life, as rich and rewarding as
it had felt at the time, now seemed as if it had been limited
to a narrow band of experience. Outside of the reality of
my earlier life were parts of myself that I had barely even
glimpsed.

Leaving turmoil and ambivalence behind, we establish
our own directives. Instead of doing only what society
requires, we focus on what is personally meaningful. We
may seem selfish; in fact, we are preserving the essence
of our true selves. By reclaiming the most valuable parts
of ourselves, we have created enduring power. Now we
can give to others in a genuinely healthy way, and we can
give to ourselves as well. For the first time in our lives, we
are concerned for our own survival. We want to nourish

and minister to ourselves — now that there is a self worth caring about, worth fighting for.

In a recent interview, journalist Studs Turkel asked thirty-four-year-old Peggy Terry what brought out her sense of adult solidity. "I think you become an adult when you reach the point where you don't need anybody underneath you — when you look at yourself and say 'I'm, okay the way I am,' " said Peggy.

To express our new status we don't don a new hat as do the Dogon people of Mali, but we sometimes change our names. Debbie becomes Debra; Donny matures to Donald. Much to her divorced mother's chagrin, a forty-one-year-old psychologist took the last name of the father she hadn't seen for more than twenty years. Sylvia, forty-three, also the child of divorced parents, rejected her father's Jewish surname in favor of her mother's Native American heritage. Sandy, the depressed housewife, became Sandra, the adult college student and announced that she no longer felt the need to charm her way out of situations. "No more cutesy stuff!" she declared.

Something has changed, and we feel the difference — it is on a strictly feeling level. There is no outward, observable behavior change, but we feel solid and this solidity is permanent. There is a new awareness of self and of others. We have gone through a crisis and have integrated our inner and outer selves. We have changed our attitudes and actions. Now we recognize our responsibilities, but we are not afraid to be playful when it is appropriate. Our new, meaningful selves integrate play and work, accommodating inner feelings and society's demands.

Our neuroses simmer down, and we accept them better. We haven't really lost them; we've learned to live with them. We synthesize and integrate parts of ourselves that have lain dormant for years. Perhaps this is why Freud gave up analyzing people older than thirty-five, when he claimed that certain aspects of personality were crystallized and no longer able to change.

Since we are focused more on pleasing ourselves than on pleasing others, we become more creative. Some take up painting. Others may begin to write. Still others may pursue a professional dream that has long been relegated to the back burner. After my own transition to adulthood, for example, I took up the piano. In my childhood, it had been my nemesis, but today, I can appreciate its gifts.

For Joe, fifty-six, a retired auto worker, the dream was walking the Appalachian Trail. "My wife thinks I'm nuts. But I'm gonna do it. I'll get me a knapsack and maybe talk to the Sierra Club, but I'll do it. I'll start in Georgia, and if I'm lucky, I'll be writing to people from Maine. I'm going to just do it, finally just do it." And with that he broke into a smile that seemed more real and more satisfying than any I had observed before.

As with the Trobriand Islanders who have no sense of continuity between an unripe, ripe and over-ripe yam, there is a similar sense of discontinuity with the individual in transition. Once we have become true adults, we are no longer the same persons we were.

"The past seems a million years ago," says Al, forty-five, a steelworker from an industrial area near Detroit:

> When I was younger, I did everything I was told. Why did I do all those things in Vietnam? They'd never get me to do that craziness now!

Authenticity, midlife crisis, selfhood, personhood, self-actualization — call it what you'd like. The problem is that there is still no test, no real norms and no validation of who lives a more emotionally meaningful and evolved life.

5

Adult Self-Appraisal

—

I would rather be whole than good."

— Carl Jung

T he following test offers the reader an easy assessment of the main points of true adulthood. While not strictly scientific, it will give you a good indication of your level of emotional growth.

Who's Adult And Who's Not

1. When a friend reports he used to try to make others happy but now puts himself first, you —
   a. Imagine you could be like him but don't know.
   b. Identify with him.
   c. Avoid the issue or think him selfish.
2. When confronted with the issue of surviving on your own in the world, you are —
   a. Uncertain.
   b. Scared.
   c. Proud.
3. When pressured by family, friends, colleagues or authority, you stand up for your own needs and best interests —
   a. Sometimes.
   b. Most of the time.
   c. Rarely.
4. When you have an impulse to be playful or simply to amuse yourself or others, you —

a. Express that side of your nature.

b. Wish you could but don't, lest you look foolish.

c. Rule out the possibility as improper.

5. When people talk about their feelings or express sympathy for the feelings of others, you —

a. Value their confidence and concern very much.

b. Are somewhat interested.

c. Are bothered by their display of weakness.

6. When you consider the possibility of sharing your successful life experiences with others, you feel it is —

a. Desirable.

b. Important.

c. Not important.

7. When you consider the possibility of leaving behind you something to make the world a better place, you feel it is —

a. Not important.

b. Desirable.

c. Important.

8. When the prospect of your own mortality comes to mind, you —

a. Think about it — and you have grieved for yourself.

b. Don't think about it.

c. Think about it a little.

9. When prompted to indulge harmful impulses, you have difficulty delaying them —

a. Always.

b. Sometimes.

c. Never.

10. When confronted by a choice between following the rules, getting the job done, and honoring your feelings, you —

a. Generally follow the rules — and you wish others would.

    b. Sometimes go by the rules, but are uncertain what is best.

    c. Usually honor your feelings — and you wish others would do the same.

To score, add up the following points for each letter you chose:

1. b,1; a,2; c,3	6. b,1; a,2; c,3
2. c,1; a,2; b,3	7. c,1; b,2; a,3
3. b,1 a,2; c,3	8. a,1; c,2; b,3
4. a,1; b,2; c,3	9. a,1; b,2; c,3
5. a,1; b,2; c,3	10. c,1; b,2; a,3

A score of 10 to 15 indicates a true adult, 16 to 23 is an adult in process, 24 to 30 is a pre-adult.

In each life there are often highlights and turning points in the quest for adulthood. Here are some ideas that will help you think about your own life.

1. Are you an adult emotionally? If so, how and when did you become emotionally adult?

2. Name any experiences you feel led up to your emotional growing up.

To stir your own thought processes, here is an example of how one individual answered these questions: Matthew, age thirty-eight, from White Plains, New York, is a shirt salesman at Brooks Brothers in Manhattan. He answered the first one as follows:

Hmmm. Yes. I'm adult. But it hasn't been for very long. I guess I was about thirty-three when I realized that this was it, this was all that there was. My father's business failed and that was always a solid enterprise and something we all counted on. Turns out his business partner stole the business out from under him. Up until that point, I thought my dad was perfect, and we had always lived an upscale lifestyle. Then suddenly, it was gone! I wanted to go to graduate school and always thought that there would be funding from the family, but now there was no money. To make matters worse, my dad died shortly after that. I stopped idealizing him, I guess, and had to mourn him at the same time. I guess that's when I grew up. It was a real emotional time for me.

Matthew answered the second question, about other experiences leading up to his emotional growing up, this way:

I gave a solo performance of "Lady Of Spain" on the trumpet, and I didn't do well and some big kids picked on me. This occurred at about age nine. Then I was playing baseball and the ball went over my head, and these kind of things stand out in my mind. Later that day, two girls recognized me and that was nice. I think I was about sixteen. A few months later, my dog ran away, and I prayed to God. Well, the dog returned, and it gave me a renewed sense of religion — of trust and belief.

Trust and belief afforded Matthew a bigger picture of adult life. Adulthood was not about mastering a certain set of rules about life; adult life included disappointments, confused feelings and, at times, a little magic.

THE BACKS OF
ADULT CEREAL BOXES

6

When
They're Gone

---

*Subconsciously, I might
have also been readying myself for
whatever might come. My husband, I think,
really couldn't quite understand the
whole thing. I think he wondered,
who is this new person?*

— Joan Lunden,
Co-Host, ABC-TV's
Good Morning America

In the movie *City Slickers*, Patricia Wettig encourages Billie Crystal, her soul-searching husband, to "go find your smile." He goes off to a dude ranch for a week and returns triumphantly as a settled and solid "adult." Of course, she has been a Zen master of understanding, support and inspiration. Ah, Hollywood. In real life, adulthood's fallout is much more likely to take a different turn, to a messy divorce.

The social fallout of the adulthood bomb can be potentially devastating. The husband comes home one day and says, "I'm sorry. I don't love you, and I realize I haven't for some time now." It's not only the middle-aged executive who leaves his comfortable family and runs off with his secretary; it's also the wife who "can't take it anymore" and suddenly bolts.

Neighbors and relatives are shocked. "He's gone midlife crazy!" they whisper. "It's a menopause thing," they titter. They are understandably confused because the people involved are grown-ups in their late forties, fifties, sixties or even seventies who have always appeared solid and stable.

Emotional Adulthood And Couples

Although there are incredibly selfish individuals in the world, adults-in-transition are not at the head of the list.

They look selfish, but *self-absorbed with survival* is a better way of saying what they are; they have not wished this experience on themselves. Judy, forty-three, experiences the typical backlash from her family:

They just don't understand. I spend most of my time reassuring him. My husband keeps calling me names, you know, like selfish. He's now turning the kids against me. I can't continue to do this alone. I get no support from anybody. He even got my mother to phone me the other day and tell me how terrible a person I am.

Actually, the family is considerably more self-centered than Judy. For years, Judy did whatever her family wanted. It was not unusual for her to spend more than fifteen hours a day taking care of the needs of everyone else and paying little heed to her own. Although she complained and even wound up in a psychiatric hospital one weekend, no one wanted to change. They labeled Judy selfish because, in their view, she was disrupting the family system; whereas she was trying to initiate change.

Let's go back to the "old ways," her family pleaded. It did not matter that the old ways were emotionally unhealthy, for this family was not interested in emotional health: it was concerned about short-term comfort.

Despite what the family wanted, or even what Judy may have wanted, Judy's metamorphosis continued. The transition toward adulthood had begun, and having begun, it had to continue. Judy was on her way to developing a sense of self, asking questions and making important distinctions between nourishing herself and nurturing others.

Adults-in-transition begin by questioning everything and everyone. It's not simply a matter of wanting information. The little questions add up to the big one, about life's meaning. And this spiritual quest has a clear emotional component.

"Do you love me?" they ask a wife or a husband. And at the moment of asking, they are seen by the spouse as weird, confused and beset by private demons — perhaps not very lovable. Often what they are seeking is not assurance of the other's love, but reassurance in the face of their own self-doubt or even self-hatred.

Debbie is experiencing her awakening in this way:

> I know this sounds strange, but, one day, I just realized that this is as good as it's going to get. I mean, I had the realization that this is my life. I know that sounds strange, but I don't think Tim thinks that way. He's always talking about getting a bigger house and boat, as if that is what it is all about.

Tim, who hasn't yet started down the road to adulthood, is understandably stunned:

> I don't know what she is talking about. She always said she wanted a nice house and a boat. These are the things we talked about, the things we were working so hard for.

Emotionally, Debbie has changed forever. With adulthood, what you see is what you get. The transition to adulthood is permanent and irreversible. As Debbie becomes more sure of her feelings and needs, she may decide that Tim has good traits that far outweigh the bad. She may elect to wait for Tim to make his adult transition — a transition that may or may not come. On the other hand, she may proceed to some more decisive action.

That's what John has done. John, thirty, is just finishing his medical residency at a large urban hospital. He is about to bury his old self and some of the relationships associated with it:

> I asked Marty the other day if she loved me. I don't know why. Maybe, I never should have gotten married. When I met Marty, she was a nurse on the ward, and she never balked at anything I did. So we got married, and, of course,

it all changed. She wanted children, and I wasn't opposed to the idea; so the next thing you know, we had one baby and then another. But it's all too much, and I resent the whole thing. It's the albatross around my neck. I can't handle it half the time. Since she's home with the kids, she's been getting real jealous of the nurses I work with; so I stay out later to avoid her. I'm depressed and nervous all the time. I'm wondering what I'm doing with my life.

Marty, the nurse who married John, previously delighted in her status as part of a young perfect couple. Her version of what is going wrong differs vastly from her husband's:

I gave up nursing to raise my two girls. My husband is just finishing his residency, and I think someone is flirting with him at the hospital. I was a nurse there, and that's how we met. The other day he walked in and said he didn't want to go on the way it had been anymore. He never talked that way before. I thought we both wanted the same things. Now, just when he has one month to go, he's been partying with the staff. I just want us to be the couple we were.

Marty can't understand that the past is gone forever; the couple will never be as they were. As long as she persists in believing they will return to their former state and be the perfect young couple, Marty will never appreciate John's discontent. Her fantasy delays her from experiencing the inevitable disappointment of her husband's departure.

As do others in the process of becoming adults, John quickly becomes overwhelmed by everything that seems wrong with him: every character flaw, every type of behavior that is not consistent with his vision of perfection, becomes a rallying point for change.

Pam's story is another variation of the adult-couple theme. A thirty-one-year-old white, Southern Baptist mother of two, Pam was depressed. Her family physician prescribed an antidepressant and counseled her to take care of her family problem with her local minister. She says:

> *My husband doesn't understand. It's something I'm going through. I mean I spend all day locked up with the kids, and I don't even like driving the car anymore. He gets away. Every day. All day. He comes home and expects me to be happy and excited and all. But how can I be? Then he keeps bugging me . . . for sex or holding or something. Like I feel like sex? But it's not just him . . . it's everything. It's my whole life!* (She begins to sob)

Don, thirty-four, understandably perplexed by her new attitude, reports:

> *I guess this thing started about a year ago when she said she didn't know if she loved me or not. And I thought, well, I still love you, what gives? I don't know what's gotten into her. All she wants me to do is leave her alone. We never used to do things alone. Then, I guess I got scared that she was gonna leave me, so I began to bug her and that's when we got into it. I don't know what to do. Am I supposed to hang around and pay the bills and wait till she leaves?*

Couple issues are complex primarily because the process of reaching emotional adulthood is so individual, and the involvement of other people and the pressure of cultural responsibilites extends it. In general the problem is that, in our culture, we get married, have children, make careers and then grow up — not the other way around. And so conflicts among the demands of parenting, career, love life and culture make our lives extremely complex.

Parenting And Emotional Adulthood

"I'm the biggest failure in the world!" says Darlene, a thirty-four-year-old mother of two. She asks a perfectly reasonable question: "How can I begin to give to my kids properly, when I myself am such a basket case?"

What Darlene is experiencing is the withdrawal of energy from her usually frenetic child-caring pattern to a more balanced child-giving stance — one that includes her as a person. As is usual in such cases, Darlene was feeling guilty about pulling back because of her own background. Having been the victim of impoverished caretaking, she revived the deprivation she experienced as a child and assumed she was causing the same pain to her children. There's just one difference — her children have had different parents and different experiences and have emotional defenses different from hers.

Another option of emotional adulthood is to have fewer children, delay parenthood or to have no children — a growing trend among younger couples in the 1990s. Irresponsible? Selfish? Many ask themselves, how can I want children when I'm still not done growing up?

According to novelist and *New York* magazine restaurant critic Gael Greene, people view having children from many different perspectives. Those who want to start a family don't consider those options.

"Couples who decide not to have children fall into two categories," says psychologist Mary Joan Gerson of New York University, "those who make a deliberate decision and those who feel ambivalent and put it off." Her studies show couples who want to be childless are more concerned about creating things in the world and leaving other kinds of memorials. Delayers, she says, appear psychologically similar to parents — but they get a job that's fascinating and then it is too late.

Sharon Lewitt, thirty-seven, a science fiction writer, has always known children weren't for her. "I wanted an active intellectual life. I didn't want to take time out from that." And that was okay with her husband, John Irvine, thirty-eight. The Washington, D.C. couple have been happily married without children for fourteen years and say they have no regrets. The life they have built is not child-friendly, as nonwork time is spent traveling and remodeling their century-old Capitol Hill row house:

> We're both insane workaholics, and we spend a lot of time on our relationship. Is this selfish? What would be really selfish is to have kids without 100 percent commitment.

Jung once said that nothing has a stronger influence on children then the unlived life of the parent.

Careers And Emotional Adulthood

A career change is often a facet of the transition to emotional adulthood. Virginia, thirty-five, celebrated her new-found status as an adult by leaving a nine-to-five job for a freelance writing career. She tells of her experience from her new home in northern Michigan:

> I loved my life in the anthill. It was stimulating and exciting. The power was exhilarating and the sense of accomplishment satisfying. It's just that one day "having it all" no longer seemed enough. I sold the three-bedroom ranch and moved into a woodsy cabin where I write stories and letters as the mood suggests. There is time to take walks through the summer countryside and to watch the river that flows nearby. My eyes see for miles in all directions, savoring and absorbing the panorama of earth and sky. I hear birds from my bed, and all manner of creatures share this land with me.

Love, Sex And Emotional Adulthood

The Phil Tong Luang tribe of northern Thailand marry five times in a lifetime, the first marriage generally beginning at the age of fifteen and averaging four or five years in length. In Himalayan cultures the pattern is the same, and so also in many others. All our laws and religious proscriptions to the contrary not withstanding, our marriage rates are not much better.

Unfortunately, there are no clear answers on divorce, since divorce rates do not offer a valid picture of happy or healthy marriages. Marriage is mixed up with a variety of other factors, such as financial and emotional dependency, cultural or religious prohibitions against divorce, raising children and fear of entering the business world or the singles scene.

Here are some sobering statistics: About half of all marriages will end, and half of those who remarry will fail again. Both men and women can expect to spend over half their lives unmarried.

Why so few successful remarriages? According to Barbara Lovenheim's *Beating The Marriage Odds*, most of us simply will not learn from the first marriage.

Probably the most devastating news comes from a 1992 study by University of Minnesota sociologist David Olson. His research is based on an unprecedented 15,300 American couples. If there is a 50 percent divorce rate, the assumption is that the other 50 percent are happy and healthy. But Olson found that only about 25 percent of those who were still married were happy. Another 25 percent were in some need of marital enrichment. The remaining 50 percent were clearly pathological, living strictly utilitarian lives based on economics and had children who required immediate therapy.

In the 1990's people are marrying less often, delaying marriage and cohabitating — although half of all cohabitating couples will eventually marry.

How, exactly, marriage survives when the adulthood crisis begins is anyone's guess. My guess is that many affairs occur as a function of a compromise between emotional adulthood and cultural responsibilities.

An affair is one way the adult-in-transition can avoid dealing with uncomfortable feelings. Doug, forty-six, shows his confused thinking during his transition:

Something has changed. I feel different from my friends. I don't know if they've outgrown me or I've outgrown them. I look at them and they haven't changed. So I guess it must be me. I was thinking about having an affair, but I don't know who exactly with or what good that will do.

It seems that men are more prone to act out their crises, while women are more likely to become depressed. But both sexes are prone to affairs; they seek reassurance as they consider the possibility of leaving a mate, and they want to test their new sense of adulthood.

Marcie, a forty-six-year-old gynecologist and mother of two, offers another tale. By cultural standards Marcie was the epitome of success. Married when she was eighteen to Allen, a successful attorney and accountant, she raised two healthy children. Until her children reached adolescence, she was content in her role as homemaker. Then she decided to pursue a career and enrolled in medical school. Marcie completed a residency program and established a practice.

Today the children are grown, and she and Allen live in a plush neighborhood in Scarsdale, New York. They have time to travel and do the things they always wanted to do, but Marcie reports:

I was so busy just trying to get through that I never had the chance to think about it. I never had time to figure out who I was. I did come to the realization that motherhood wasn't enough for me. I was suffocating! I needed more stimulation, and I needed to breathe. Then, trying to balance being a mother and getting through medical school — to this day I don't know how I did it. Allen was good that way. I couldn't have done it without him. He raised those kids as a single parent during those years. I guess I never had the chance to think about it this much. You know, I used to feel so guilty. My parents were always telling me to marry a doctor and that I had no right to be one. I used to try to please everyone. Now, for the first time in my life, every-

*thing is slowing down, and I'm beginning to think. Who am
I really? What do I want? I mean, yes, it's a picture-perfect
story on the outside. But on the inside, something is missing.
I can't feel my life. Everything seems up in the air.*

For years Marcie did what she thought would guarantee
her happiness and success. When the outside world slowed
down and its demands became less insistent, her inner
voices grew louder and cried out that something was missing. Her life seemed great by anyone's standards but her
own. It did not feel good to her. Overwhelmed by her
feelings of adulthood, she entered therapy at forty-six to
discover what constituted adulthood for herself.

She's toying with the idea of an affair: "There's this cute
resident at work who asked me to go out with him. He's
younger and doesn't know I'm married. He thought I was
thirty-six. Does any of this make sense?"

It seems reasonable to suppose that most affairs offer
the adult-in-transition a way to test a new identity.

"I suppose the experience I had with Craig came about
because I was testing the market and myself — looking to
see if anyone understood me or wanted me if I did leave
Jim," says Denise, thirty-four, an adult-in-transition who
is outgrowing her mate.

Says Donna, thirty-six, another restless woman experiencing growing pains: "I never knew who I was before.
It seems like forever that I've been somebody's mother
and wife. My family doesn't accept me, but my lover does!"

Sometimes, the affair helps the new adult break the ties
that bind. The new adult wants an excuse to leave. Such
is the dangerous scenario Randy, age 38, describes:

*The other day it came up. My wife saw my credit card
receipts from the hotel. I should have known it was only a
question of time. I really don't care at this point anyway.*

True adults make decisions that satisfy inner needs,
moving from attitude to action. Divorce may be a short-

term answer to a long-term problem of how to live with disillusionment and the imperfections of another person. Nonetheless, most consider the possibility, and some quietly begin a slush fund — a separate savings account to financially back a move out of the house. "As soon as I graduate, I will make the move," says a calculating Terry, age thirty-three.

What To Do?

There are very few dos and don'ts as the process of reaching true adulthood unfolds and moves forward. Yet many couples make life worse for themselves by not following the three guidelines.

Don't Fight It

You must surrender to the process. Delaying or avoiding doesn't work, and depression seeps out anyway. Obsessive people, so-called control freaks, seem to have the most difficult time adjusting, since they are in an uphill battle that can't be manipulated. Denying it is like pretending you're an ostrich and putting your head in the sand. As in Zen Buddhism, the way to minimize negativity is to move with and not against an inevitable force. The only way to beat the bronco is to ride it out.

If you're close to someone who's in the process of transition, try to be supportive and understanding without letting yourself be abused. The adult-in-transition needs help, and you can help best by keeping open the lines of communication.

Don't Take It Personally

This is the most difficult concept to uphold since we are speaking about the person who is your betrothed, your significant other, your spouse. The adult-to-be is not undergoing this process on purpose to make your life miserable: he or she is doing it because emotionally there is a very real process going on. The transition to adulthood has little to do with a spouse — it has to do with an individual's emotional development.

Get counseling by a specialist in adulthood and aging. Friends and spouses rarely understand what is really happening. Most are quick to judge, and advice from friends and relatives who are highly biased in one way or another will do more harm than good. Try to seek advice from someone who has been through the process and has some understanding of what has occurred.

Don't Wait For The Old Ways To Return — They Won't

The old ways and the old spouse will never return. One thing is certain: having grown up, the new adult can't regress. It is up to the other partner to make adjustments.

One of the biggest mistakes most spouses make is to believe that the new adult will change back to what he or she was. I have seen one woman in therapy for over two years and another for over a year waiting for their men to return emotionally (and physically). No one returns emotionally.

The behavior of adults-in-crisis may vary as they test newly emerging parts of themselves, but they will eventually find what works for them. These new traits will become permanent fixtures of their personality. Rarely are they running off to Mexico with the secretary or moving in with the aerobics instructor. In most cases, it is simply that they retreat to an uncomfortable emotional distance.

Only Two Options

The good news is that there aren't too many options to confuse an already confusing process. The bad news is there are one of two choices: Either you put up with the situation or you don't.

Adopt A Wait-And-See Approach

"What am I supposed to do?" one spouse asked angrily. "Just sit around and pay the bills and wait and see if she sticks around?" It is a valid question since estimates of the process suggest it lasts an average of 2.5 years, with an unknown outcome.

One of the most difficult adult development cases I have ever seen was a thirty-two-year-old, very dependent woman and her anxiously attached spouse. Her messages to him were, "Give me some space, but don't go too far away . . . maybe the next room or something. And by the way, can you drive me to the mall?"

Her spouse was an angry, all-or-nothing kind of guy (perhaps justifiably in this circumstance) who couldn't tolerate ambivalence. His messages back to her were, "I don't want you to leave me. But I can't stand not knowing if you're going to leave. I'd rather end it than go on not knowing."

At one point he asked me if he should wait longer to see if she was staying. It is a question without any correct answers. The best I could do was to answer with more questions: What are the options? What can each individual tolerate? How good was the marriage to begin with?

Withdrawal is one way to deal with the seemingly impossible demands of the world. Jane, a forty-one-year-old homemaker and mother of three, is no longer interested in the structure of marriage and family:

> *There are irreparable wounds that gape and continue to bleed. I can't go back to repair and console Jim. There is no magic suture, no magic drug to make everything better. The pain is much too deep for any anesthetic to touch. The deepest scar is that of betrayal. My body is no longer in my control. I have been abandoned to the whims of my soul.*

Her husband, Dick, a forty-five-year-old insurance agent, is confused. As his spouse moves toward her true adulthood, he has to live with the isolation:

> *What in the world is going on with her? Janie has always been a little on the fringe. But this time is different. She doesn't do any housework. I come home and the place is a mess. I'm doing most of the cooking and the kids just keep asking me what is going on with their mother. I can't really tell them because I don't have a clue myself!*

The new adult is trying to align inner and outer worlds to accommodate a dramatic emotional shift. There is nothing anyone can do to stop or even slow down this emotional process. Yet, there are definitely several things that may help weather the emotional storm.

Not every relationship bears salvaging, and one can't negotiate what was never there to begin with. The husband who married because he thought it was the right thing to do may leave after he determines his emotional needs. Social pressure from parents, religion or work are no longer sufficient reason to continue a loveless marriage.

Meanwhile, the woman who married a provider and discovers she can support herself — and never really liked her husband — may seek a divorce once she has figured out that she can survive both emotionally and financially. For Jenny, twenty-seven, a flight attendant, the decision was even simpler. "My husband is so boring. I realize now, I'm not right for marriage."

Get A Divorce

I believe that emotionally outgrowing another individual is probably the main reason for divorce and frequently the adulthood crisis is the catalyst. And the only thing that truly lasts is true emotional companionship. Both men and women who grow up may no longer require the services of the emotional parents they married. That's what

Alex, fifty-four, an elementary school teacher, realized. His second wife couldn't protect him from his worst enemies — alcohol and gambling.

"I have no idea why she stayed with me as long as she did," he admitted. After she divorced him, he married another woman who was simply a modified version of his first two wives. Frustrated with her efforts to control him, he divorced her and was about to begin a fourth relationship exactly like the others when he stopped himself. For the first time in his life, he slowed down, quit drinking and gambling and learned to befriend himself. Now, at last, he is ready to enter intimate relations.

Divorce is always a distinct possibility for any couple. In the adulthood crisis it becomes more distinct.

I have had some patients who stay and some that leave. Sometimes separations are helpful, as in Woody Allen's *Husband And Wives*, where, after a brief separation, the good aspects of one relationship are seen to outweigh the bad.

No one really stays in a marriage out of a sense of duty and responsibility. People stay because it works for them. There is a sense of companionship and an emotional "dance" that simply works enough.

Ultimately, the shift to adulthood results in emotional health and stability. An adult relationship is emotionally active and reactive — both partners are free to listen to and express their feelings. As André Gregory says to his friend, Wallace Shawn, in Louis Malle's classic cult film, *My Dinner With André* :

> But I do think you have to ask yourself with total frankness, is your marriage still a marriage? Is the sacramental element still there? And I mean, it's a very frightening thing to have realized that suddenly . . . that, my God, I thought I was living my life, but in fact I haven't been a human being — I've been acting. I hadn't really learned what it would be like to let yourself react to another person from moment to

moment along a chain of feeling that can change from one second to the next. And you see, if you can't react to another person, there's no possibility of action or interaction.

There are individuals who are unwilling to grow up emotionally and who will never make the transition to true adulthood, and to true adult relationships. Are you involved in a relationship with a grown-up who cannot grow up? Or worse, are you one?

7

Grown-ups Who Don't Grow Up

—

*The fact is my fortieth birthday
was fast approaching and I still did not
feel grown-up. Even if . . . I had put on a
jacket, I still would not have felt like
a grown-up at the party.
But how old are you supposed to be
before you become a grown-up
in your own head?*

— Bob Greene,
syndicated columnist

B y the time this book goes to press Bob Greene will probably have had his adult crisis. But others are delayed. And still others — eternal Peter Pans or Wendys — may never experience true adulthood. Why?

The answer is not well understood, and what is understood tends to be complex. For example, in his autobiography, *Final Analysis,* psychoanalyst Jeffrey Masson recounts how he leaves the horrific politics of the psychoanalytic community and his career in order to become his own person. But shedding our belief in the culture's version of happiness is only part of the process. Defeating our own demons is also part of it.

Such is the adult journey of feminist Gloria Steinem. Born to a dysfunctional family in Toledo, Ohio, Steinem had little in the way of adult role models while she was growing up. Her mother popped pills; her father overate. As a child, she says, she often felt neglected, deprived and insecure. Food was a comfort, as she juggled work and school and caring for her sick mother, all the while carefully hiding the family's secrets. When she got older, Steinem continued her caretaking, substituting a magazine and a movement for her parents. She did succeed, but that was all on the outside. On the inside, a different picture emerged emotionally. She admits:

Like a recovering alcoholic, I'm a foodaholic who can't keep food in the house without eating it. I'm still trying to stay healthy one day at a time.

Steinem believed that she could deny her childhood traumas, but years later in therapy, she discovered that her distorted body image and her habit of binging were linked to a troubled past. Now healthier, she has acknowledged with her book, *Revolution From Within*, that "the inner revolution is to realize our full self."

Steinem recognizes that career ambitions — and even the achievement of a successful career — can thwart adult development just as surely as emotional problems can.

Defenses: The Wild Card

Emotional defense mechanisms may be the biggest wild card in determining who becomes an adult. Defenses are our protection against perceived threats. Although we don't have a complete understanding of defense mechanisms, we know that they help us maintain a balance between what we can cope with and what we cannot, and that they enable us to manage stress and to marshal resources against a particular problem. Some of us, however, create too many defenses and use them to disguise inner needs.

People who are more defensive than they need to be are covering their tracks, trying to admit no weakness. Some use denial to stay in control, talking and acting as though some disturbing aspect of reality did not exist.

Some use conformity to social values as a defense: by way of the mechanism they can ignore or bury impulses that seem to go against social conventions. Frequently, the most solid citizens are the most rigid individuals. They may have become official do-gooders, spending much time and effort on behalf of the community. Perhaps they have adopted their parents' ambitions for their own. They enjoy society's rewards for their efforts. But they rarely feel fulfilled or satisfied because they have lost touch with their emotions. Personal feelings terrify them. In truth, these individuals lack personal insight and any real emotional depth.

Ed, sixty-eight, a retired laborer, is intent on doing what is right: "Look, I'm the generation that believed what the man says goes. Am I right? Sure I'm right. Now my wife is upset and says I don't listen to her."

Some people defend themselves by expressing an impulse in action to avoid thinking about it. Teenagers do this frequently; they tend to act first and deal with the consequences later. Impulsive and highly anxious people also rely on action to gloss over feeling states. In general, men tend to act out when faced with the crisis of their inner growth, often by starting an affair, as Bobby, a thirty-six-year-old factory worker, explained to me:

> Sure I didn't come home that night. I was pissed at her. And so I didn't feel like answering to her. I was getting loaded with my friends at the bar, and I knew if I didn't phone by eleven PM she'd be pissed. Sure enough, she shows up a half-hour later and says for me to come home. I tell her off. And I knew, she'd just bitch at me if I came home. So I stayed out.

"He was there with another woman; he must be going through that midlife thing!" his wife Brenda, thirty-five, concluded. Bobby later confessed that he was there with an old girlfriend whom he had been seeing thoughout his five-year marriage. It was all right, he believed, because he hadn't had sex with her since his marriage. They were "just friends."

Overly defensive people are generally at risk for delays in adulthood. So are those whose personalities are disordered in some way; they are too angry, too passive and conformist, too scared, too rigid, too self-absorbed and too anesthetized.

Bob, fifty-one, a Los Angeles investment broker, married to a disturbed woman, felt he was living in chaos:

> *She had a boyfriend twenty years younger and she was in therapy for this or that. She said she was just trying to find herself. She was always trying to find herself, going to this therapist or that one. The latest thing was that she was into channeling and then wanted to start giving money to a group in Seattle. I just couldn't keep up with her. It was always something. One day she just came in and said she wanted out. Tore me up inside at first. Now I think that I'm a helluva lot better off.*

Unfortunately, therapy and counseling will usually not help much because these individuals are not open to change. Success in psychotherapy requires the same ability to be open to experience and the same vulnerability that must precede the metamorphosis to adulthood.

Eternally Young

Sometimes acting out mimics an adult crisis so closely that it is impossible to tell the difference. The primary difference is that an adult crisis is going somewhere in terms of internal identity, whereas general acting-out behavior merely reflects personality.

There are those who use childish behavior to attract attention and work out conflicts instead of feeling their uncomfortable feelings. Although there are theories about why some individuals choose to be kids forever, few have been tested.

One view suggests that whether we admit it or not, we all struggle with a desire for eternal youth. While the true adult eventually achieves a balance between the child and the adult, many people cannot. Perhaps they are unable to tolerate the demands of adult life.

In the Jungian concept, the eternal girl is as natural and as American as Gidget. She is the *puella,* the girl next door, the archetypal sweetheart, the ideal wife, like Donna Reed in *It's A Wonderful Life,* Marlo Thomas in *That Girl* and Mary Tyler Moore in *The Dick Van Dyke Show.* Marilyn Monroe, Paula Abdul, Kim Basinger and Vanessa Williams offer sexier, but just as idealized, versions of women who are "forever your girl."

The eternal girl is invariably an emotional chameleon. Whether she models herself into what others expect or defiantly rebels, she is too busy reacting to others to develop her own voice. Bonnie, forty-nine, now divorced from her philandering physician-husband, demonstrates such an accommodation. She is uncertain of her role. She contemplates a face-lift to help maintain a part of her past identity — being pretty for men:

> *I grew up in the South where men knew how to take care of women. There was none of this angry women stuff. I like the idea of being taken care of by my man, and I'm ready when he needs me. I guess I'm pretty old-fashioned when it comes to how a man should treat a woman. The other day I was thinking about what I need to do in order to keep a man. A little plastic surgery here and there couldn't hurt.*

Frequently, the eternal girl starts as the dutiful, dependent daughter, then marries a controlling man, a "daddy," and defies him. Unless someone or something makes her change, she remains a helpless girl for the rest of her life.

The armored amazon is often contrasted with her, but this female analogue of the macho man may be simply the eternal girl within, who defends against her own vulnerability. An ambitious overachiever, the hard eternal girl carries a chip on her shoulder. She likes fighting for a cause, being in control and laying down the law. Financially independent and successful on the outside, such women do not appear to have a spontaneous bone in their bodies. Inside, they secretly cry out to be nurtured and cared for.

Since much of what goes on is invisible, we can only hazard a guess at the defense mechanisms involved. They can be defined as the mental actions that prevent us from actually experiencing our most dangerous thoughts or wishes. When they are weakened, we become more vulnerable. With insufficient internal defenses and negligible external support, collapse of meaning is inevitable.

Most of those who seek treatment for difficulties encountered while passing into adulthood are struggling with hidden issues that obstruct their growth. They need help in discovering who they are. Kim's tale demonstrates some of the complexities.

At forty-two, Kim was caught between a ticking biological clock and her adult self. The eldest of three girls, she had been a hard-working, straight-A student. She studied management in college so that she could join the family's business after graduation. By the time she was thirty-five, she had risen to a top managerial position in the male-dominated furniture business. She began to experience headaches, fatigue and insomnia. She felt the world's weight on her shoulders, and she grew increasingly despondent and depressed.

By the time Kim entered psychotherapy, she was feeling trapped by a compulsion to be perfect in her work and by her inability to develop her emotional life. She remembered her childhood as unhappy: her parents had wanted a son first, not a daughter. Her father counted on her to live up to his expectations of a boy, and when she did well, he rewarded her. He took her into his business and spent time with her, something he did not do with Kim's sisters.

In reality, Kim was living her father's life and not her own. During the day she lived up to his ideal of hard work and achievement. At night, she led a rebellious alternative life. Realizing this discrepancy in the course of therapy,

Kim was able gradually to nurture her own creativity and emotional needs. She enrolled in an astrology course and pottery and art classes, activities her father criticized as impractical and self-indulgent. She began to meet new people, and although she still had to struggle with her tendency to be a perfectionist, she began to feel energetic and hopeful about life. For Kim, differentiating her needs from her father's expectations is cumulative; the more she does, the more her own meaningful adulthood emerges.

The eternal boy is the *puer,* Don Juan, the consummate lover. While traditional feminine values encourage women to be girls, society does not tolerate the eternal boy. Attracted initially by his impassioned sensuality, women are soon repelled by his inability to make commitments and follow through. Such is the dilemma of Ray, thirty-seven, a playful deliveryman:

> *You know my girlfriend walked out on me because she got wind of Gail, the one I met on my route. You know women. They sort of smell it or something. I admitted it to her. I want her back.*

Joe, thirty-three, works in television production and drives a Porsche. But success hasn't brought him personal happiness. "I've gotten to the top of my field," he says, "but I'm just no good in relationships. I just can't make a commitment."

Ray, Joe and many men, including the writer, spend their lives searching for perfection in a partner and at the same time want freedom. But as the Eagles' song *Desperado* suggests, their freedom itself has become imprisoning.

Another type, equally frightened of feelings and reluctant to commit himself to any structure, is the diffused person who likes to keep things vague. Straddling the fence, agreeing with everyone or keeping things simple ensures safety. Graham, in Stephen Soderbergh's film *Sex, Lies And Videotapes,* has pared his life down to the basics:

Well, see, right now I have one key, and I really like that. Everything I own is in my car. I get an apartment, that's two keys. If I get a job, maybe I have to open and close once in awhile, that's more keys, or I buy some stuff, and I'm worried about getting ripped off, so I get some locks, and that's more keys. I just really like having the one key. It's clean, you know.

Disengagement effectively delays adulthood, but it does not eliminate discontent. Even such a person cannot escape the haunting sensation that there must be more to life.

The highly touted macho man is all performance and little substance. There is still plenty of cultural support for men who "just do it," as the Nike advertising campaign proposes. Whether these men are making a million dollars or jogging with the boys, they are similarly caught up in the traditional role of men. They are afraid of their feelings and, for the most part, miserable.

The men's movement, championed by a number of psychologists and Jungian theorists, including Herb Goldberg, Sam Keen and Robert Bly, may hold some promise for the eternal boy's development. These leaders in the field of psychotherapy have legitimized help for macho men, who have been notoriously antitherapy.

Character-disordered people are at risk for never attaining true emotional maturation. Many are caught up in a vicious cycle of the past. What did your parents do? What did your parents not do? Major disappointments of early life can thwart the process of maturation. In some cases the pain in early childhood can be too great to face, and so borderline personality-disordered people can be unable to leave behind their past assaults. But true adulthood can be attained only by leaving the past behind — or at least living in tandem with it.

8

The Spirit And Adulthood

---

*The spirit of play,
the spirit of eternal youth is the
foundation and beginning
of all real life.*

—R. G. Collingwood

*Free your mind and the
rest will follow.*

— Funky Divas

I n some sense, true adulthood is childhood recaptured. Popular psychology has recently — with great fanfare — discovered the inner child. Yet my research and the investigations of countless gerontologists supports the fact that as long as we are healthy emotionally, physically and socially, we are ageless.

In childhood our emotions were real and not culturally filtered. As children, we were in touch with our basic needs and not interested in status. In childhood there is a sense of connection with others and an intuitive appreciation of a universal soul. Or, to put it another way, in childhood we were more connected to our essential human spirit.

In true adulthood, we recapture our basic vulnerability and connect with the mystical élan and spirit in each of us. This spirit is ageless and genderless. It transcends time and space, and it is free of worldly attachments.

Jung recalls this sense of child as a creative life in his autobiographical *Memories, Dreams and Reflections:*

> *The first thing that came to the surface was a childhood memory from perhaps my tenth or eleventh year. At that time I had a spell of playing passionately with building blocks. I distinctly recalled how I built little houses and castles, using bottles to form the sides of gates and vaults.*

Somewhat later I had used ordinary stones with mud and mortar. These structures had fascinated me for a long time. To my astonishment, this memory was accompanied by a good deal of emotion. "Aha," I said to myself, "there is still life in these things." The small boy is still around and possesses a creative life which I lack. But how can I make my way to it?

Several decades later and a continent away, Jane, the suburban Detroit homemaker, reflects on a similar struggle to integrate these various feelings of her inner child:

There was a time much too brief, but oh so sweet, when that little girl, now in the persona of woman, truly believed in the happiness and goodness alive in herself and the people who supposedly loved her. Too soon she learned differently. Childhood dreams rapidly became adult nightmares. All that was hoped for now was hopeless. Given time she would adjust and adapt; which she did. She did not, however, ever forget those gentle times when love was sweet and the world was good. I'm entitled to those dreams, those feelings that comprise my little Rock of Gibraltar. I want to embrace them and hold them close to my heart — for therein lies my strength.

As we become emotionally adult, we re-integrate our repressed child parts. We may take up piano lessons or painting again. We may begin to write creatively. We may move on to careers that are more consistent with our childlike underdeveloped parts, producing a stronger, more solid and comprehensive self. We are no longer fighting a hidden enemy within. As true adults we can re-examine our values and determine our inner feelings. The storm is over; we can relax and play.

Through his work with dolphins, wolves and children, play specialist O. Fred Donaldson has simplified the magic formula for play. In a recent book, *Playing By Heart*, Donaldson suggests that kindness, trust and enchantment are childlike qualities that we long to recover as adults. Donaldson suggests that the quest to recapture these qualities requires —

(1) an openness to experience life's mystery, (2) a capacity for fearlessness to meet the unknown and (3) a willingness to practice steadfastly. Fearlessness moves one to all, openness moves all to one. Without openness there is no ground of potentiality to support fearlessness. Without fearlessness there is no means of actuality to reveal mystery. Through practice, openness and fearlessness become kindness.

Play is about a flight of fancy and a whit of wisdom — play is a vocation and a quest requiring trust, fearlessness and action. Play is being aware and taking care without appearing to do much of anything.

This integration of spirit and practice in useful and effective action is described as a "way" in Eastern thought. It is based on kindness — a realization that we are one of a kind.

Anthropolgist Ashley Montagu has written extensively about neoteny — how being childlike is helpful in maintaining agelessness. He has identified the following neotenous traits:

Playfulness, imagination, creativity, experiment, flexibility, openmindedness, humor, joyfulness, laughter, tears, optimism, song and dance, honesty and trust, compassion, intelligence, curiosity, exploration, sense of wonder, resiliency, friendship and love, sensitivity, the need to know, to learn, to organize and to work.

Related work in psychoimmunology, the investigation of the mind-body relationship, is still a fairly recent area of research. And the scientific study of play is even more recent. But to experts the pursuit of play is serious — deadly serious. "Play may be the body's front line of defense against illness and pain," says University of Rochester psychoimmunity specialist Robert Ader. Documenting the relationship between play and the immune system, Ader showed how cells of the immune system take their cues from chemical activity in the body, which, in turn, is triggered by our responsiveness to outside stimuli.

On the West Coast, neuroscientist Marion Diamond and her colleagues at the University of California, Berkeley, demonstrated an important positive relationship between play and agelessness. She placed mice that were 766 days old — roughly equivalent to seventy-five-year-old humans — in an understimulated environment. Not unexpectedly, they began to grow listless, and their capacity to learn new skills diminished. In short, they showed all the signs of what we call growing old. Given toys and novelty items in an enriched environment for their last 138 days, they learned to do new tasks more quickly, and they lost all signs of aging. Autopsies of these mice showed evidence of positive biological changes: larger neurons and increased glial cells.

Another Berkeley study, on older adults, found that those who keep play at the forefront perceive their lives to be rich and happy.

Other studies show that playful adults have more close friends and tend to be more socially involved than their more somber counterparts. In a Yale study of 7,000 adults, respondents who had strong friendship networks outlived their socially disconnected counterparts.

How can you tell true adults? They play, and love.

True Adults Play

Most people in our culture don't know how to play. Take Betty, eighty-one, who in spite of her advanced age is vigorous and considers golf her true play. One day as Betty and her friends were about to tee off, Betty paused to take a Valium. "Is everything all right?" her friends inquired. "Of course," she said, "I just like to take a little of the edge off before I play."

How sad. Here is a woman out with her friends for an enjoyable morning, and she cannot play without first sedating her competitive self.

Long before we became competitive and responsible adults, we were children, and children have a natural ability to play. In the process of growing through childhood and adolescence toward adulthood, we learned to discard many aspects of ourselves in the name of maturity — but we discarded too much. Part of our task as adults is to permit the natural, childlike tendency to play to re-evolve. The ability to play and express humor, to experience joy and feel laughter, mark the true adult.

On the other hand, Ron, fifty, a business manager for a major automobile manufacturer, assumes that adult life is all work. "Play? Ha! My job doesn't allow me to at all." But Ron's inability to play does not stem from his job — it's a product of his acculturation:

> We were a good German Protestant family. You know, fairly strict, the kind where you weren't permitted to oppose your parents, where we couldn't talk about feelings, and certainly weren't supposed to have fun. Besides, I had to be the serious one since my brother, Bob, was always getting into trouble and making my parents worried sick.

For his next vacation, Ron promised to do something "wild." At long last, he wanted to learn how to play.

Play is hope and optimism making way for curiosity. It is a sense of awe and wonder that feeds a basic need to know. "Perhaps the saddest loss of all," says Montagu, "is the gradual erosion of the eagerness to learn." He goes on to say:

> Most adults stop at any conscious effort to learn early in their adulthood, and thereafter never actively pursue knowledge or understanding of the physical world. It is as if they

believed that they had learned all they needed to know by the age of eighteen or twenty-two. At this time, they begin to grow a shell around their pitiful store of knowledge; from then on, they vigorously resist all attempts to pierce that shell with anything new. In a world changing so rapidly that even the most agile-minded cannot keep up, the effect of this shell surrounding a person is to develop a dislike of the unfamiliar. The hardening of the mind — "psychosclerosis" — is a long distance from a child's acceptance.

True adults have the ability to play as passionately as children throughout their lives. As French symbolist poet Charles Baudelaire said, "Genius is childhood recaptured."

When we play, we temporarily take leave of our self-possessed world and abandon social conventions. Altered states of consciousness, very often artificially induced by drugs, may be the mind's natural attempt to create a feeling of play when we have been deprived of it for too long.

Creativity

True adults play, in a way, to look beyond themselves and to leave a mark upon the world. Playful thinking can be the catalyst for creation in the field's of fine art, music, literature and scientific invention; it can also manifest itself in kindness, consideration and generosity.

Play can evolve with the birth of children — the ultimate creative act. Diana, thirty-three, says:

My daughter is beautiful and is almost three now, and I feel that she's changed my life. I'm a different person. I get home at the end of the day and just unwind with her and play.

True Adults Develop Finer Sensibilities

Often it is only when we are faced with death or tragedy that we understand that molding ourselves to society's image has been a mistake.

Compassion

In 1991, Lee Atwater, George Bush's hardball campaign strategist and chairman of the Republican National Committee, died from a brain tumor. He was thirty-nine. Shortly before his tragic death, he shifted gears and found a new level of adulthood. He apologized:

> In 1988, fighting Dukakis, I said that I "would strip the bark off the little bastard and make Willie Horton his running mate." I am sorry for both statements: the first for its naked cruelty; the second because it makes me sound racist, which I am not. Mostly, I am sorry for the way I thought of other people. Like a good general, I had treated everyone who wasn't with me as against me. After the election, when I would run into Ron Brown, my counterpart in the Democratic Party, I would say "Hello" and then pass him off to one of my aides. I actually thought talking to him would make me appear vulnerable. Since my illness, Ron has been enormously kind — he sent a baby present to my daughter, Sally T. He writes and calls regularly — and I have learned a lesson: politics and human relationships are separate. I may disagree with Ron Brown's message, but I can love him as a man.

Even the hard-nosed Atwater came to realize, as he looked toward death, that his life had been missing emotionally adult thinking; had he been able to do it again, he would have had "a little [more] heart, a lot [more] of brotherhood."

Passion

"Without passion, man is a mere latent force and possibility," writes social critic Henri Amiel. Passions are the driving force of willful intentions. Without finding and acting on our passions, we can never be fully adult. When we are able to play, to be empathic and to create with passion — when we are able to live with body and soul, and to give ourselves fully to whatever tasks we feel are right — then we come alive and finally experience the meaning of true adulthood.

In Leo Tolstoy's *War And Peace*, Pierre, the main character and a member of the nobility, is captured by Napoleon's army and undergoes terrible deprivations. He is surrounded by cruelty and suffering and sees no hope for the world. But one fellow prisoner, an elderly Russian peasant, is full of zest despite the travails. He meets every event that befalls him with good cheer, and he passionately continues to care.

Confused by what he sees, Pierre one day asks him, "What is the secret of your happiness and contentment?" "Secret?" asks the peasant, "the secret is to live!"

Some time later, the peasant is killed. But his example sets Pierre on a course of introspection that culminates when he vows to live life to its fullest, never again to follow the dictates of a decadent society, and to follow his own passions, wherever they may lead. He has become a true adult.

Nurturance

The highest function of true adulthood is nurturance — the ability to be empathic and put aside one's own needs, to reach out and give. When an individual nurtures because it is culturally esteemed — that is not true adulthood. True adults have achieved the state of being able to nurture themselves — and so they can nurture those around them.

Sue, aged twenty-nine, describes her attempt to nurture by sharing:

This girl at work got married the other day. She's all of twenty-one and came to me crying about some nonsense. I tried to tell her, to talk to her and tell her what she was doing. You think she'd listen? Nope. I tried. When I was that age, I thought I knew it all. Now I'm older and I realize that I don't know anything. She's a good person, and I'll try again.

PART II:

AGELESSNESS

9

The Soul Has No Age
(*L'ame n'a pas d'age*)

—

We'd be a baby every day.
— Response from first grade students when asked:
What would happen if there were no time?

One day you go to your friend's wedding.
One day you celebrate the birth of their kids.
One day you see one of their kids driving and
One day those kids have kids of their own.
One day you meet at parties and then
at weddings and then at funerals
It all happens in one day.

— Richard Cohen,
Syndicated Columnist

When adults find that they have more in common with an eighty-year-old than with an eighteen-year-old, they change their notion of *old*. Older folks suddenly become, if not contemporaries, then at least relative equals. Mark Twain spoke about his growing-up experience by understanding that the know-nothing father of his youth had somehow become incredibly wise by the time Twain was thirty.

Most of us are, at some point, struck by an awareness that we are aging — and the word *lifetime* takes on a new meaning, as it did for this thirty-two-year-old physician:

> *Suddenly came the realization that many have accomplished much more than I have in a shorter period of time. I have spent half my life screwing around in school and career and haven't even lived my life yet. What a joke!*

But the human mind does not like to remain in a permanent state of dismay, and so most of us find a way to accommodate to aging, as has Harvard philosopher Robert Nozick in a charming way:

> *I don't like to think I'm much more than halfway to the end of the major thing I am engaged in. There is leeway to decide what this is, though, and so I adjust boundaries accordingly to create new midpoints. "Not yet halfway through life" — that served until the late thirties or the age of forty;*

"halfway through work life after college" got me to the age
of forty-five; "halfway after college to the very end" gets me
approximately to now. Next I need to find still another mid-
point not to be much beyond, and I hope to continue making
these adjustments at least until old age, which, too, for a
while I will be no more than halfway through.

The new boundaries that we create may seem whimsi-
cal at first glance, but in fact they really help provide a
positive outlook for the future.

Another experience of subjectivity in aging is recounted
by fifty-four-year-old divorcée Isabel Davis, who describes
her first-time dating experience with an "age-appropriate,"
sixty-year-old suitor:

> *I felt as if he were too old for me. The first time he came*
> *to the door, I had an urge to say, "My mother's not home*
> *right now." My reaction was not objective; the man was only*
> *six years older than I. It was not fair; he did not look that*
> *old. (My children thought he looked fine for me.) But I had*
> *been married to a younger man — I was used to what he*
> *looked like. I was not ready for older-looking men, and I*
> *didn't know yet that most older-looking men were not ready*
> *for me — they had passed through the stage of women their*
> *own age with their first wives, usually years before.*

When "Old" Begins

What would happen if there were no age markers, no
birthdays or records of aging were kept — if we had no
memories of the number of years we've been here?
Quipped baseball great Satchel Paige: "How old would
you be if you never knew how old you was?"

Physical aging is no longer synonymous with feeling
old. Norman Vaughn, eighty-six-year-old Alaskan adven-
turer, competes annually in the Iditarod, the 1,150-mile
dogsled race that turns the fittest thirty-year-olds into
haggard wrecks. Psychiatrist Viktor Frankl, well into his

eighties, still scales the peaks of Europe. Seniors run marathons, while early retirees become couch potatoes by their mid-forties.

In the past, middle age melded into old age after children moved out of the house and became financially independent. Today, with people living longer, and in smaller or outside families, adults are sandwiched between generations. Nests may be vacated sooner or later than expected or not at all, making previous signposts of middle age barely perceptible.

For many years, sixty-five marked the cutoff between middle age and old age. Most people retired at sixty-five and started to collect Social Security and pension checks. Now some "retire" at fifty-five only to embark on a new career. Career military people typically retire from service after twenty years, sometimes at the age of thirty-eight. Those who collect a pension or Social Security benefits may still continue working in some capacity into their seventies and eighties. In reality, there is no empirical measure of old age.

My research in age identification reports seventy-year-olds who feel thirty-five subjectively, and thirty-five-year-olds who feel seventy. The thirty-five-year-olds who felt seventy were less healthy in the domains of physical, emotional and social living than were the others.

According to two of my studies, we feel on the average at least seven years younger than our chronological age, and the older we get, the more that difference increases. In a 1985 survey, people said they felt on average eleven years younger than their real ages, and by 1990 the difference had increased to fifteen years. Psychologist Carin Rubenstein, after making a survey of more than 9,000 *Glamour* magazine readers, found that their concept of age was defined emotionally. More than half no longer defined themselves by age, even though they worshipped youth — their ideal age ranged from the middle to late twenties.

Education and income play a role in how we view old age. Working class Americans in general marry earlier, retire earlier and, not surprisingly, see old age earlier than do their better educated and more financially well-off counterparts. In Rubenstein's study, 48 percent of low-income respondents, as against 30 percent of middle- and high-income respondents, stated they were "senior" before the age of sixty-five. The stress associated with having less education and money apparently makes people feel older faster.

Unfortunately, researchers and theorists alike continue to perpetuate the idea that if you don't feel your chronological age, you must be denying reality. One psychoanalyst recently stated that feeling young was an "illusionary misperception." And it is only recently that these "experts" have accepted the idea that age denial could be healthy. One research team interpreted its findings in this way:

> . . . *seeing oneself as younger may be a denial of reality, but a denial that may be necessary for good psychological functioning. It may, therefore, be unwise to attempt to break down denial in the elderly, in terms of helping them accept their physical limitations and aging.*

Sometimes, the so-called experts must spend energy, time and money before reaching conclusions that were obvious to everyone else.

In fact, after re-examining all the research and theories of the past thirty years, I have concluded that there is no evidence that our feelings of subjective age are invalid. I am convinced that people who feel subjectively younger than their chronological ages are people who simply feel good — and "feeling good" is correlated statistically with being healthier, more socially involved and emotionally sound — specifically, feeling in control and having a greater sense of purpose.

Another widely accepted notion is that all older adults experience time as slowing down. Yet when I separated out nursing home respondents from actively involved, community-dwelling respondents, time was not the same for both groups. Not surprisingly, emotionally and physically healthy and active people do not experience time getting faster each year, until there is a sense that it is just whizzing by. Essentially all active people say the same thing about time — that there never is enough of it!

Emotional Oldness

So when does old age begin? Some say old age begins when poor health creates major limitations. Recent surveys, however, show that half of all seventy-five-to-eighty-four-year-olds report no such limitations. Even among those over eighty-five, one third report no limitations. According to one Lou Harris poll, there is no concensus on how to estimate old age. Close to half the respondents picked a number (varying widely), while the remainder defined oldness by circumstances (health failure or retirement, for example).

But just as there is no set time when adulthood begins, so there is also no set time when old age sets in. An eighteen-year-old crackhead; a materialistic, emotionally empty suburban matron; a corporate hustler; an underachieving, alcoholic factory worker — all may feel equally old because they have all lost a sense of themselves and are simply going through the motions.

My own experience of growing up suggests that age is emotional and more a state of mind than anything chronological. As a child, I had a special relationship with my mother's father. Hardworking and unsophisticated, my "Papa" always had a twinkle in his eye, a spring in his walk and a no-nonsense attitude. He worked with his hands, making his living as a furniture salesman, one day achieving his own version of the American dream by becoming a store owner.

An ambitious, younger business partner forced my grandfather out by rigorously applying society's sixty-five-and-out rule. Almost overnight, Papa began to age before my eyes. Within six months of his forced retirement, he appeared different. Gone was the twinkle in his eyes, the lift in his step, the lilt in his voice. He looked vacant and hollow. His booming voice grew tremulous and uncertain. He withdrew into what we call old age.

Since he was nearing seventy, geriatric specialists called him pseudodemented, an ugly term reserved for depressed elders. Their condition is generally treatable with a course of antidepressants — but these drugs made Papa even more listless. His next round of treatment included antipsychotics, which only made him dopey, deadening his spirit.

"What is the point?" my granddad argued. "Nothing matters anymore or in the long run." And he was right. His psychic lifeline had been severed, and his body followed suit. He became so used to looking down and avoiding eye contact that his body began to hunch. His walk slowed to accompany his mental hesitation. He seldom spoke, and when he did, his speech was less and less clear. His body was obviously undergoing some massive disintegration. It took but a brief bout of pneumonia, and then he died.

"Why?" I asked. What had caused such a drastic change in such a short time? The answer was not simply old age because for every older person who physically lets go there are others who do not. Not all older adults became so alienated and devitalized.

I further investigated the meaning of *old* and found the process of thinking old can occur in substance-abusing young adults, in chronically depressed housewives, and in middle-aged auto executives who are suddenly disenchanted with the corporate criteria for success.

"We are not old," writes French feminist Simone de Beauvoir, "it is the *other*, the stranger within us who is old." I have met old forty-year-olds and young eighty-year-olds. I have seen physically healthy individuals with old attitudes and handicapped or ailing ones whose disability does not interfere with their feelings of youthfulness.

Martin Grotjahn, a famous analyst, documented his own turning old. At seventy-five, after a series of heart attacks, he simply gave up. Reports the newly old doctor, "I was now content to just sit . . . watching the leaves fall, in no hurry to get anywhere." But his lack of emotion was possibly recuperative. In fact, some studies show that people who feel old reverse their aged feelings when they become less burdened.

I have finally concluded that the subject of age has less to do with physical characteristics and society's expectations than with emotional vitality. "Being old is not really a problem," says age-defying comedian George Burns, "thinking old, now that's a problem."

Emotional Youngness

Through my investigations, I have come to realize that being old means surrendering what we value most — our essential selves, the most meaningful aspect of who we are. An old feeling or sensation acts as a distress signal that the essential part of ourselves has grown alienated, depressed and ready for death. Oldness happens to all of us at times when we venture too far from the vital reality that is us.

Many choose to give up in different ways at various points in life. In this sense, growing old is a synonym for *surrendering*. We develop a kind of premature aging syndrome, a trigger ready to shoot us into old age at a moment's notice. But we cannot see it because premature aging is consistent with the prevailing culture's definition of maturity.

Accelerated aging may begin as early as childhood. "Grow up," we are quick to tell our children; "feelings have no place here." We submit to religious strictures and bow to the demands of family and friends. We suffer humiliation and depression when we lose a job or are rejected by the girl or boy of our dreams.

Gradually, we begin to get numb. We stop feeling our feelings. We rely on the words of others — friends, parents, society — and we work beyond our capacity in an effort to achieve some kind of meaning.

We attend funerals. We realize we are not rich or smart. We realize that we have done wrong and been on the receiving end of others' wrongs. We realize we are mortal. We listen and care too much for what others think. All of this is quite normal. But with so many assaults, part of us simply gets old, becomes frail, and withers and dies. A wall rises between us and reality. "Homo analgesia" was philosopher Sam Keen's term.

These attacks on our human spirit occur whether or not we make the transition to adulthood. But those who do not become adults experience the pain of loss and the grief of mortality without remedies. They become conservative, rigid and stultified in their thinking, old men and old women, because once they have ceased to grow they have become old. Frozen in time, prematurely aged — what the Thai's call *ching suk kon haam:* ripe before ready.

Who Are The Ageless?

Who are the ageless? They are all of us who feel our lives. They are all of us who have prevented our ageless spirit from withering away. They are all of us who have made a decision to pay attention to our subjective experiences and make them the driving factors of our lives.

The ageless are those who preserve the spirit of the child. They are inquisitive, curious and playful. In fact, says Montagu, the ageless exhibit these childlike traits. They have ageless emotions.

Ageless Emotions

Emotions are timeless. If something makes us angry, it's the same anger at the age of five or fifty-five. Anger is anger, sadness is sadness — and science is busy validating these notions. University of Delaware psychologist Carrol Izard has investigated primary emotions by analyzing infants' facial expressions and their corresponding moods. His findings suggest that we are all wired for the same fundamental emotions that ensure safety and self-protection. Our faces register fear, sadness, anger and several other "survival" emotions: for example, eyebrows raised and pulled together signal fear, and a lifting of the inner part of the eyebrows indicates distress.

Clinical observations further support Izard's findings. Patients who cry while describing an event are revealing that this is an emotionally hot topic. Patients who pound on the arm of the couch while talking are also providing a significant clue to emotional depths. Clinicians use these, and other emotional expressions, as therapeutic guides in determining treatment routes.

The clinician knows that primitive emotions are so age-free that an eighty-year-old can speak of an emotionally charged childhood experience as if it occurred yesterday. In one sense, because our primitive emotions remain unchanged through time we never grow up. Fifty-five-year-old siblings may squabble over an inheritance in exactly the same way children squabble over toys, manifesting exactly the same emotions.

In another sense, this continuity of feelings can be a source of positive action. A ninety-year-old great grandmother can wish to look pretty for a prospective eighty-six-year-old suitor down the hall: in her mind's eye, she is in her forties or even in her thirties. At sixty, *Esquire* magazine writer Thom Morgan reflects on the ageless part of ourselves: "Hopefully, if there's an afterlife, it will be with this ageless inner eye that never grew old, that spends eternity looking back at time."

The Essence Of Agelessness

"What was essential was invisible to the eye," observed the fox in Saint-Exupéry's *Little Prince*. And, what is essential, of course, is the heart. The heart is our emotional life, our passions; it is what truly matters and what we intend when we filter out the needs of society.

We all start off this life with passion and intention — the trick is to maintain them in contrary and hostile surroundings. Julie Francis Hunt, forty-eight, an elementary school teacher in the Midwest, writes of her passions and those who block it:

> It is fear that causes them to move back or to strike me because I think deeply and feel fully. This behavior has caused me to fear myself and pull away or cover up what matters to me. I am shattered by their reactions to me and feel less than them, when in fact I have and am more than they. I have a gift that they do not understand — in trying to make them understand I have followed them, away from me. I must now trust me and find my way back to my center, my true self. I must not listen to their misunderstanding. I must not need them to understand nor listen to their words that would pull me into the dark, away from my fire, my being.

We Americans, who pride ourselves on rugged individualism are, in fact and for the most part, strongly prone to bow to cultural convention. Unfortunately, our culture prizes production over creativity, conformity over individuality and material success over emotional contentment. Any deviation from this schedule suggests that we have failed to get with the program.

Living by one's passions and authentic feelings is the ultimate nonconformist stance, and yet it is what is required to become a true adult and to maintain a life of agelessness.

There is fear among some moralists and persons of particular religious persuasions that living by one's own passions is dangerous — to one's self, to society and to God's law. But there is a passage repeated in different words in many scriptures throughout the world to the effect that "spontaneity knows its own morality." This means that when we pay attention to our hearts, to our deep feelings, we cannot but lead moral lives.

It is interesting to observe that those who have had near-death experiences almost without exception choose to live the passionate life. Characteristically they manifest decreased fear of death, increased openness and desire to learn, more playfulness, greater appreciation of life, an encompassing respect for and love of people and nature, enhanced empathy and compassion and an increased desire to understand their relation to the Creation.

These individuals who have come close to death are unanimous in affirming their agelessness. Chronological age is no longer of importance to them; they are too busy living each day to its fullest.

We are entering a new age of aging, one that will free us from the previous shackles of time and permit us to live a healthier, happier and more meaningful existence.

This is an exciting time in gerontology. We are dawning on a new understanding of age-free selves. All we need to do is give ourselves permission to begin dealing with one another based on our individual, inner feelings rather than outward appearances and chronological age. Getting the culture and political climate to catch up is a much bigger problem.

10

New Age Aging

---

*All their life whether they
are thirty or whether they are fifty —
they still continue to be that child
though they were no more.
Once they have recovered him,
once they have merged with him,
it does not matter whether they
are thirty, or fifty or even eighty.
They have escaped from age.*

— Simone de Beauvoir,
from *The Coming Of Age*

An Ageless Culture

O ur society is now beginning to focus on the quality of life. And because we are looking younger, we may be moving toward an ageless society. At a recent symposium on aging, gerontologist Bernice Neugarten commented on recent changes in age norms:

We have become accustomed to seventy-year-old students, thirty-year-old college presidents, twenty-two-year-old mayors, thirty-five-year-old grandmothers, fifty-year-old retirees and sixty-five-year-old fathers of preschoolers.

Indeed, the average eighty-year-old today bears no resemblance to the grandparent of yesteryear. Sylvia Herz, at a recent American Psychological Association Annual Meeting, similarly observed, "The activities of today's seventy-year-old are equivalent to those of a fifty-year-old a decade or two ago." Higher survival rates at birth, better nutrition, healthier lifestyles and medical advances may be creating physiological agelessness. We live well into our seventies and early eighties, and centenarians are not nearly so rare as they once were. More and more adults are living longer, extending middle age and reducing the span of old age.

Soon it will be quite possible to stay in roughly the same physical shape from late adolescence to the age of eighty. After that will come a brief period of ill health that will become known, perhaps, as "fragile elderhood."

As a group, the young-old (chronologically in their sixties and seventies) are healthier and wealthier than their predecessors. They command more marketing attention because of their savings and paid-off mortgages, which translate into buying power. Clearly, in the United States, chronological age is on its way out and agelessness is in. Makeup ads show three generations of women who look like sisters, and it is no longer unusual to see television commercials showing octogenarians holding hands at a local restaurant.

Herb, a favorite eighty-two-year-old uncle of mine who lives in Los Angeles, made the family proud by appearing as a cool senior for a recent Keds sneakers advertising campaign. He made other commercials for Chili's and McDonald's — positions that were virtually closed to him ten years ago.

In reality, there have always been individuals whose flame began truly to burn in the second half of their lives. Henry Ford began the Ford Motor Company at the age of forty. Winston Churchill was prime minister at seventy. Leo Tolstoy celebrated his seventieth birthday by biking twenty miles and then making love to his wife. It has always been there, but now we are accepting the new look — physically and mentally ageless older adults.

When John Updike writes about the antics of his aging hero in *Rabbit At Rest*, he no longer equates age with disengagement. We have begun to view older individuals as people rather than as statistics. With increased awareness has come political power. There is a permanent gray lobby in Washington, D.C. — one senior activist organization is called the Gray Panthers. And the American Association of Retired Persons is 28 million strong.

Aging is coming of age. We are becoming more psychologically sophisticated and mentally healthier than ever before. The more adult we become, the more we focus on our meaningful selves and grow up emotionally. We are increasingly meeting the challenge of the times and changing our lives, unwilling to take emotional early retirement, unwilling to disengage and wait to die.

Television talk shows, always a reflection of what is important to our culture at a given moment, are focusing on feelings and on a subjective understanding of who we are. Phil Donahue, Oprah Winfrey and a number of other hosts discuss a variety of emotional concerns, including the psychological agelessness of older adults. They introduce examples of successful older adults and show us how it is possible to age without acting old.

One such vibrant older adult, John Cowles, former director of Harper & Row Publishers and editor of the *Minneapolis Star,* started a dancing career at sixty-one, when most are preparing for retirement. A newspaper account of Cowles's new life describes him —

> . . . *wearing royal blue tights and rolling around on the floor, a balding and gray-haired man of considerable wealth and status, rehearsing with an ensemble of gorgeous young dancers a post-modern work at the end of which they and he and his sixty-five-year-old wife will be nude.*

Our lifestyles are trying to catch up to our new agelessness and emotional adulthood. Delayed or postponed marriage is a good example. In general, we have fewer marriages. The "never married" category has swelled from 5 percent to 10 percent of all adults in the United States. An astounding 25 percent of men and 17 percent of women aged from thirty to thirty-four have never married. That is almost triple the 1970 rate. The average age for first marriages — twenty-seven for men and twenty-five for women — has increased by four years since

1960. On the other end, a record number over sixty-five marry each year — 65,000 people.

After raising children and attaining some degree of financial security, older adults are less willing to compromise their independence. Older women who discover autonomy after the death of a husband are particularly reluctant to commit to another relationship. As Betty, eighty-four, says:

> *Me marry again? Ha! Not at this point in the game. Taking care of a man again? What for? My husband is gone almost ten years and I have enough to live on. Sure I get lonely at times, but I'd never marry. Take care of them when they get sick? Ha!*

Sixty-eight year old *Esquire* magazine contributer Robert Sherrill recoils at the thought of accepting the old age culture. He writes:

> *I head for the saloons (restaurants down here), with low hopes. Maybe that pretty waitress at Devines will yield to my charms. Even a blind hog finds an acorn every now and then. Like many another vagabond, I ricocheted back and forth across the country, whipped on by work, hope, or curiosity or some restless demon. After the sailors of yore, I have (or had) a society in every port. Saloons were where your societies were. I know almost no one my own age. You are becoming the New Invisible Man, with only a boon buddy or two as witness. Isolation is setting in. Time has been at its sure work, picking off kin here, a friend there; a wife here, a lover there. It sends you down one fork of the road and those you love down another. First thing you know, the solo life has been achieved.*

Ageless Grandparenthood

The traditional rules of thumb and conventional wisdom no longer apply. The cause is, in part, economic, as adult-age children are returning to the parental nest to recover from broken marriages, to seek financial assistance or to enlist support in raising their own children. For example, Bill, aged sixty-seven, retired early, just before his youngest daughter returned home with her three-year-old son:

> *I was all set on moving to Florida with my wife, and then Jimmy and Barbara moved back in. Didn't like it at first. But what are you going to do? I mean I worry . . . I think this is a permanent arrangement here unless she gets married again. I worry, too, about what's going to happen when we are in our seventies and, you know, one of us gets sick. Then there's the financial. We planned on retirement for two, not four!*

Ageless Work

Ten years ago it was rare to see an older person working behind a fast food counter. Today, a grandmother clears tables along with her teenage coworker. Companies look to older groups to fill service jobs, and older adults frequently elect to work past sixty-five. Dorothy, seventy-one, needs to work: "I don't know how a person makes it these days. I just get by as it is."

Many of us no longer want to work just to earn more money or to get ahead. The reasons we choose to work suggest our desire to escape from the age trap, according to a Harris poll. Workers and those who are looking for work are almost as interested in feeling young as they are in money.

Bill, seventy-three, for example, wants to work: "I was looking forward to retirement after all the time of working. But I was bored out of my mind. Even if the government takes my Social Security, it's worth it just to feel productive."

Ageless Relationships

Barbara Lovenheim's book, *Beating The Marriage Odds*, re-examines a controversial Yale-Harvard study — the one that suggested that a forty-year-old woman had a better chance of being killed by a terrorist than of marrying. When re-analyzed, the data showed that men and women both had equal chances of remarrying.

Currently, both men and women can expect to spend about half their lives unmarried. Half of all women will divorce and remarry within five years. Women will tend to marry younger men (one-to-five years younger). On the other hand, we are cohabiting more. According to the Census Bureau, the 439,000 unmarried couples in 1960 swelled to almost 3 million in 1990. Half of them will eventually marry.

As we become more emotionally adult and ageless, we are designing the decision to have children around our emotional development, and so we are having fewer children and having them later. In 1970, 4 percent of women having a first child were thirty or older; by 1987 that figure rose to 16 percent. The good news for those who would postpone parenthood is that "older parents have . . . already sorted out pretty important things" and tend to be more altruistic, according to Miami University gerontologist Robert Atchley.

Since child bearing years have been extended, there is more time to spare. At the turn of the century menopause began when a woman was in her mid-thirties; now it begins at approximately the age of fifty, with a seven-year variation factor. Because we are biologically extending middle age we are changing our norms of what is appropriate with regard to age.

With more people approaching the maximum human lifespan, the question of which spouse will die first becomes statistically answerable — those who have reached their seventies are well aware of the dramatically imbalanced male-to-female ratio.

"Sure I'm worried that he'll go before I do," says Eve, seventy-eight. "But what am I going to do? I'm the only one of my friends who has a husband. All the rest are widows." The fact is that men begin dying earlier than women from birth on. The greater fragility of males is reflected in birth rates — more girls born than boys — and all through life in males' higher death rates. The female X chromosome is a key factor in certain antibodies. Also, estrogen, a significant female hormone that controls reproduction, appears to maintain the integrity of women's health. It specifically guards against atherosclerosis; testosterone does not. Apparently, diamonds are not the only best friend a girl has.

Once people resolve the issue of childbearing, age differences become less and less important. "Friends ask me what I'll do when I'm in my sixties," says Janis, thirty-seven, who is married to Alan, fifty-five. "The idea that I'll wind up as a twenty-four-hour nurse is not real appealing. On the other hand, if we have ten good years together, we've doubled the national average! Besides, we've had our children."

As we become a more ageless society, the barriers to marrying a partner much older or younger are breaking down. Here is an interesting chart showing the relation of age discrepancy to happiness in marriage.

	Relative Age Of Spouses		
	10+ Yrs. Younger	Same Age	5+ Yrs. Older
Wives			
Happily married	83%	86%	90%
Unhappily married	17%	14%	10%
Husbands			
Happily married	91%	87%	81%
Unhappily married	9%	13%	19%

Source: Brecher, M. (1984) *Love, Sex And Aging*. (N = 4,246)
Reprinted by permission of Little, Brown.

Notice that where the husband is older, a higher percentage of marriages are happier. In other, more controversial research, the older spouse is seen to be the one most likely to benefit from the ageless relationship. Chronologically older spouses report more happiness and live longer than their counterparts who are married to spouses of their own age.

Agelessness And The Culture

Agelessness may never be completely possible in the strictly physiological sense, but we are moving in that direction. As the adult state extends itself, we become closer and closer to an age-free lifestyle. With it comes the exciting possibility that the outside culture will align itself with our feelings of agelessness. At that point, an age-free culture becomes not just a philosophical notion or an attitude, but a context that allows us to live our lives fully and freely, without the limitations of age prejudices.

An age-free culture could more closely align responsibilites — driving, voting, juvenile incarceration, legal parental responsibility, marriage and retirement — with the transition to true adulthood than with chronological age markers. For example, everyone has known youngsters who are mature enough to drive before the age of sixteen and others who shouldn't be driving at any age.

It is in the primal state of agelessness that we return to the child within, and we play, instead of repressing the best parts of ourselves. If, as Plato writes, "the gods were happiest when man played," why do we do so little to please them? Dutch historian Johan Huzinga observed, "More and more the sad conclusion forces itself upon us that the play element in culture has been on the wane since the 18th century, when it was in full bloom."

Regardless whether our culture advances enough to support the freeing of ourselves to follow our passions, as individuals we have no choice. For those of us who make the successful transition to adulthood, whether society can accommodate our newfound freedom is moot. Once we are true adults, and once we are living on the basis of our feelings and passions, we cannot go backwards. For the power behind our metamorphosis is the very lifeforce itself.

PART III:

—

AGING

11

The Body Electric

Well the trick is simple,
to die young
as late as possible.

— Ashley Montagu

No one dies of old age anymore. Now doctors understand the specific causes of death and have pinpointed conditions and symptoms that are generally age-related. They know, for example, that in time we all run the risk of acquiring various illnesses, such as hardening of the arteries, not unique to older people, but prevalent.

All Systems Are Not Equal

Now we know that not all bodily systems age at the same rates. In fact, at any given age, some of our systems and parts are quite young while others are old even before we have grown up.

Sight

Beginning in childhood, the lenses of our eyes start losing elasticity, and by our late thirties or early forties our ability to focus on close objects becomes discernibly limited. Similarly, the pupils of our eyes become smaller and less able to open and close rapidly, making it more difficult to adapt to changes in light, especially at night. Fine print becomes more difficult to distinguish. By the time we are in our fifties and sixties, driving at night elevates itself to the level of annoyance, and the first pair of bifocals may be ushered in. As we approach our seventies and eighties color intensities subside, and we have a 50-50 chance of developing cataracts.

Today, outpatient surgery to correct farsightedness is successful 60 percent of the time, and it's improving each year. Cataracts are not nearly so dangerous to our sight as they once were.

In a sense, we already have ageless eyes in that prescription glasses have generally allowed us to have reasonably good eyesight until the end of our life. Now we are getting closer to being able to manipulate our natural lenses so that we can dispense with the external ones.

Hearing

Changes in hearing are not generally noticed until we are in our fifties or sixties. Even then only about 30 percent of the older population is affected. However, about 15 percent of all adults will be dramatically affected by hearing loss by the age of seventy-five. In general, if you can just hear something at a range of 40 feet in your twenties, the range will have declined to 32 feet as you approach your fifties, and to 23 feet in your sixties; when you are seventy, the voice that was audible at 40 feet must come to within 15 feet. The greatest loss occurs in hearing high-pitched sounds.

Keeping your distance from loud sounds (80 decibels or more) is the best way of preventing hearing deficits. (Whereas about 60 decibels is normal for conversation, the noise of a busy street corner can reach 80 decibels and the noise on a subway can reach 100.)

There is good news for those who have hearing loss. New technologies in hearing aids have finally been able to screen out background noise. And with high technology, hearing aids will probably become invisible very soon. Look for hearing-aid implants, possibly by the year 2000.

Touch

The research on touch suggests some negative changes after we are well into our seventies. Cold and warm thermoreceptors, which maintain body temperature, are the main concern. Older adults have lower body temperatures than they did at the age of sixty and have a more limited comfort zone. Small wonder the Sunbelt states show the highest in-migration of older adults.

With advancing age, pain is experienced with progressively less intensity, but the bad news is that pain is our index for avoiding certain dangers. Exercise, exercise, exercise to maintain thermoreceptor health.

Taste And Smell

The acuity of our tongues and noses declines as we age. Our sense of taste declines much more than our sense of smell. In fact, recent testing on subjects ranging from a six-year-old to a ninety-four-year-old revealed only minute differences in their ability to distinguish odors. But if your older aunt's eating habits have included red-hot chili more and more as she gets older, don't be surprised. Our sense of taste changes radically as the number of active taste buds declines, and so we desire greater intensity of flavor.

As with all organs and bodily parts, taste and smell function on a use-it-or-lose-it basis.

Hair, Skin And Teeth

About 30 percent of the population, both male and female, will notice gray hairs by the time they are in their thirties, and all men show at least some signs of hair retreat. Male pattern baldness increases statistically with age to about 50 percent of the male population by the age of fifty, and 60 percent by the age of sixty. Minoxidil is only effective about a third of the time, but there is word that several new discoveries to retard hair loss will be coming up within the next decade.

Wrinkles and loss of skin tone are still our primary visual method for determining age. Wrinkling begins quite young, even in one's twenties. By the time we are in our late thirties and early forties, vertical frown lines appear, even when we are not frowning, as does the smile line from nose to mouth, even when we are not smiling.

Even though we may gain weight as we age, the fat under our skin decreases, causing wrinkles to grow more pronounced. Our skin loosens everywhere we don't want it to. Jowls form under the chin; the earlobes begin to enlarge and droop, as does the tip of the nose.

All laboratory signs show that sun damage to skin and the effects of aging are identical. The best medicine for the former is prevention: avoid the sun.

If both your parents aged without significant wrinkling, chances are you will too. But new products are coming out, such as a synthesized melanin to replace the naturally occurring skin pigment that protects against the sun's rays. Within a few years, we should be able, with prudent habits, to retard aging of the skin.

The strength and condition of aging teeth is considered to be genetically influenced, but there are some established norms. By the time we are in our twenties, if we fit into the average, we will have one tooth missing and eleven fillings. Those numbers double by the time we enter our thirties and then level off after the age of forty, to twenty-eight fillings and from five to ten teeth missing.

Water fluoridation, introduced in this country as early as 1947, is still controversial. There is evidence to show that the additional fluoride in our diet increases the brittleness of teeth, causing greater tooth loss in adults.

Teeth decline in quality and quantity, but that may be not so much a function of age as of plaque accumulation and neglect. Research is now under way to determine why certain ethnic groups exhibit no apparent tooth decay. And if past improvements in dental health continue, there is no reason we should not be able to retain near-perfect teeth throughout our lives.

Stomach, Kidneys, Lungs And Heart

In terms of food and beverages, you can get away with anything in your teens and twenties, practically anything in your thirties, and absolutely nothing from your forties onward. The culprits are less stomach acid, an esophagus that stays open when it shouldn't and shuts when it shouldn't, and oversensitive bowels. By the time the forties hit, we eat smaller portions, but doing so is helpful, since we have a tendency to hold weight more easily. More fiber and more water will help promote more effective digestion.

Since your bladder shrinks with age, elimination is necessary more frequently. Some kind of problem with the prostate gland troubles 60 percent of men over fifty. But new, improved ways of alleviating prostate troubles have been developed, including a new medication that shrinks the enlarged prostate in two-thirds of the cases.

As early as the age of thirty, a high percentage of both men and women will endure painful kidney stones. Athough their incidence may be minimized by using fewer dairy products and drinking more water, probably one in five persons will still have to live with them. Effective medications, as well as a kind of sonar blasting, will be more readily available in many communities.

Lung capacity is a good indicator of biological age, since the lungs grow weaker with time — though for the majority, the decline is not noticeable. Lung capacity is at its height at the age of twenty and declines by approximately 1 percent a year. Aerobic exercise and certain vitamins, such as carotene, have been proven to be effective in slowing lung, and also cardiovascular, disorders. Again, exercise is vital.

Despite our advances to date, approximately 20 percent of men and 10 percent of women will experience heart attacks by the age of sixty. Angioplasty, medications or bypasses are effective treatments, but the best treatment, of course, is prevention. A high-roughage, low-fat balanced diet and exercise helps. Good news for nappers: in a Greek study, men who took naps were 30 percent less likely to suffer heart attacks than those who didn't.

Ageless Bones, Muscles And Weight

"Oh, my aching back," is a frequent complaint as we age. General joint stiffness and a characteristic discomfort in the spinal area after exertion are common among aging Americans. So is osteoporosis, a calcium-deficiency problem common in postmenopausal women. Here, the key to improvement is moderate but frequent exercise, with appropriate food supplements, especially calcium.

New hope from Emory University on the drug etidronate has been promising. Etidronate has been found effective in reducing spinal fractures and actually appears to increase overall bone mass. High-tech synthetics are also making their way from the laboratory, and osteoporosis sufferers may soon find themselves getting used to synthetic cartilage replacements. Recently scientists at Washington University changed muscle to bone in laboratory animals using osteoginin — with great implications for 20 million osteoporosis sufferers.

Muscle strength begins to slowly decline after the age of thirty. In men, the muscle mass that declines will eventually be replaced by fat. In women, a decrease in subcutaneous fat gives the appearance of muscularity. Preventive exercise such as weight or resistance training and aerobics may do much to delay declines in muscle strength and tone.

Body Weight

Unless we take stringent measures, most of us gain weight with age. There is some controversy regarding how much weight is healthy. The addition of one pound a year after the age of twenty-one is all right according to the old school of thought. But a growing number of gerontologists are suggesting that even moderate weight gain increases the risks of diabetes, as well as cardiovascular and other medical problems.

The king of weight reduction is UCLA's Roy Walford, whose lean and trim persona and personal restricted daily caloric intake of 1,000 calories speak for his self-discipline. Walford's notion is simple. Severely restricted caloric intake, together with close attention to balanced nutrition, produces greater longevity, an increase in lifespan of as much as a 50 percent. When the caloric intake is restricted daily to about half of the usual allowance, increased health, energy and longevity are seen in laboratory animals. But so far, there are no studies of humans — except by Walford himself.

Whether or not Walford's just-say-no approach can increase longevity in humans is not yet certain, but Walford, approaching seventy, is by far the healthiest looking gerontologist at the Gerontological Society meetings when compared to his colleagues of the same age. Perhaps Walford's dream of extending the maximum lifespan to 200 years from its current 120 can one day be realized.

Nutrition And Food Supplements

It's not only how much you eat but also what — and by now most of us are aware of the benefits of a low fat, high fiber diet. In a recent Harvard survey of 88,751 nurses, those following their standard red meat diets developed colon cancer 2.5 times more frequently than did their meatless counterparts. A Cornell University study of 6,500 Chinese goes even further, linking all sources of animal protein, including fish, to heart disease and cancer. Our rates of heart disease among men are about 67 per 100,000; the Chinese rate is 4 per 100,000. The good news is that a highly touted Japanese mushroom that supposedly tastes like steak is soon to be imported into the United States.

Besides, high fat meals may depress a man's sex drive. Recent research at the University of Utah found a 30 percent decrease in testoterone levels after a high fat meal.

While the virtues of bran have been well publicized, the next nutritional star on the horizon may be carrots. Their beta-carotene seems influential in preventing heart disease and cancer. If further studies corroborate beta-carotene's effect, carrots may become a standard breakfast food.

Garlic increases the cancer-fighting ability of the immune system and significantly reduces cholesterol. If further studies support current findings, then garlic and carrots may come to be injected as standard additives into certain foods, such as breakfast cereal and breads. The good news here is that the garlic will be deodorized.

Teas seem unlikely candidates for promoting longevity. But certain green teas have been found to contain a compound that reduces lung tumors.

Gerovital H-3, the Romanian spa remedy and wonder drug, does indeed make people feel younger, since it contains a mild antidepressant, but it has never stood up to rigorous American standards on longevity testing.

After *60 Minutes* reported that red wine reduced heart attacks and strokes, American imports from Burgundy and from Bordeaux swelled. What the TV report failed to mention was that Washington, D.C., a city of red wine consumers, still holds the highest cardiovascular disease rate in the United States. The lowest rates for heart disease occur in Japan, where red wine consumption is virtually unknown. Incidentally, the telling ingredient in red wine is also to be found in red grape juice, but no one has stocked up on that.

Drugs . . . Drugs . . . Drugs

Deprenyl, the Canadian drug developed to treat Parkinson's disease and thought to increase the maximum lifespan of 115 to 145 years, is being prescribed by some physicians to those who dare to try it. There is no direct evidence of its effects on humans yet.

Arthritis sufferers may receive the proverbial shot in the arm in the form of rumalon and arteparon, made from cow cartilage, trachea and lungs. These drugs have halted osteoarthritis in rats and dogs and seem to reduce pain in humans.

Resistocell, an all-purpose rejuvenator produced from embryonic sheep cells, stimulates the immune system while it diminishes the signs of aging and reduces certain cancers. The only side effects are occasional pain and swelling at the injection site.

Three European oral antibiotics — phenformin (England), metformin (France) and buformin (Germany) — have increased the lifespan of mice by 25 percent and reduced all forms of cancer. At the prestigious Petrov Institute of Oncology in St. Petersburg, Russia, gerontologist Vladimir Dilman used phenformin to reverse age-related declines in metabolism and immune function. His result — sixty-year-olds with the immune functioning of twenty-five-year-olds — suggests an important link between immune system and metabolic functioning. These drugs have been withdrawn recently in this country because of side effects they produce in diabetic patients, but the Food and Drug Administration (FDA) will most likely reapprove their use soon.

Chromium in the diet of experimental mice has doubled their lifespan. And a family of organic compounds found in most fruits and vegetables, quionones, seem to be involved in connective tissue and brain metabolism, protecting against ongoing body cell damage, invigorating brain cells and slowing down normal aging.

Recent work at the University of Wisconsin has made the human growth hormone, or HGH, famous. The process of HGH goes something like this. Generally, skin and muscle tone begin to decline at about age thirty. (Lean body mass declines at an average rate of 5 percent a decade until the balance of fat to lean is about 50-50 by the age of seventy). When a synthetic form of HGH was ingested along with a diet of 25 percent protein, 50 percent carbohydrate and 25 percent fat by twelve elderly men for six months, their body fat declined by 14 percent and their muscle mass increased by 9 percent. Growth hormone levels of people aged from sixty-one to eighty-one approximated those of forty-year-olds. The problems are the unknown effects of long-term therapy and a current tab of $14,000 a year.

The Aging Brain

There is a decrease in the overall size of the brain with age, but that doesn't appear to mean much, since there is no apparent correspondence between shrinkage and brain functioning. According to T. Franklin Williams, director of the National Institute on Aging in Bethesda, Maryland, life after thirty is not all downhill: "Even though we lose brain mass, we continue to develop more cross-connections between cells, which may be more important than the actual number of cells," he says.

Our understanding of the brain is still in its infancy, and Alzheimer's disease is a case in point. Twenty years ago, senility was a catchall term commonly used to describe what was considered a consequence of normal aging. Most gerontologists now believe that senility is not inevitable and that Alzheimer's, one extreme type of this disease, occurs because of a genetic insufficiency.

A gene associated with heart disease, APOE-e4, occurring in 31 percent of the general population, has been implicated in the protein build up associated with Alzheimer's dementia: Duke University researchers have found a single copy of it in 64 percent of a group of Alzheimer's patients.

Memory research debunks some myths. We lose a little recent (primary) memory as we age, but we appear actually to increase our long-term (secondary) memory. As a result, we rarely forget a thirty-five-year-old argument, but we may not remember our next-door neighbor's name.

Brain Enhancers

Research on IQ scores suggests that some decline in abstract reasoning ability accompanies the aging process. Those who use this part of their brain on the job — accountants, engineers and mathematics teachers — feel the loss most keenly. But there appears to be no change in conceptual or verbal skills, and wisdom — that is, the ability to use these skills with perspective and balance — does increase with age.

In San Francisco, it is possible to walk into clubs — Toon Town or Big Heart City — and order the latest drug and vitamin cocktail to stave off the effects of brain deterioration or age-associated memory impairment. An estimated 100,000 people nationwide are regularly injecting "smart" drugs such as DMAE, Vasopressin and Piracetam to boost alertness and short-term memory. Users report results that range from enhanced creativity to enhanced sex.

But do smart drugs really work? The answer is a qualified yes — but so far they work best in laboratory rats. If you are human, smart drugs do not yet exist. There are, however, some intriguing findings on the horizon. A synthetic antioxidant, called centrophenoxine, seems to increase mental stamina. BCE-001, an offshoot of centrophenoxine, raises cell function in older animals to levels even higher than those in young animals. Studies report that animals that receive BCE-001 live about a year longer than those that do not, but the results on humans are still unknown.

Phoshatidylserine, which leads the army of drugs used against Alzheimer's, improves learning and memory and produces a youthful electroencephalogram (EEG) in animal studies. Hydergine helps keep the brain metabolism from falling below levels observed in healthy young adults, giving older adults the appearance of improved cognitive function, memory, social behavior, mood, alertness and sleep, but geriatric psychiatrists, lifespan researchers and physicians are all waiting for more proof.

Ageless Mind

The mind tells an entirely different story; at no point is psychological growth compromised by age. In other words, psychological growth and biological declines are unrelated. In terms of personality, gerontologists have failed to find any evidence to support the idea that individuals grow rigid in personality traits as they become older.

The tie between mental and physical health is still emerging from the realms of mystery and faith healing. The pioneer work of Carl Simonton and the popularizing of the body-mind connection by Deepak Chopra, Bernie Siegel, Dean Ornish and others have presented countless cases in which a will to live and an ability to play have combined to effect some kind of cure or remission of disease.

We do have evidence that the emotion of anger, along with tense, self-centered, competitive behavior, makes for a Type A proneness to heart disease. Psychologists Lydia

Temoshok and Henry Dreher suggest in *The Type C Connection* that repressing all emotions in conjunction with appeasing, self-sacrificing behavior makes for increased cancer risk. Ideally Type Bs, or the most healthy personalities, cope most effectively by expressing emotions and meeting and responding to their own and others' needs. In a related study of emotions, researcher H. Aaron Katcher at the University of Pennsylvania found that the mortality rate of those with pets was one-third less than those without pets.

Ageless Sexuality

We do not know a great deal about sexual interest and performance in relation to aging. Orgasm frequency peaks somewhere around the age of nineteen for men, who report an average of 3.19 orgasms weekly. Women appear to reach their sexual prime much later in life, and report more frequent orgasms in their thirties and forties than in their earlier years.

As men age, they require greater stimulation and more time to become aroused. Their erections are less firm, and the time between orgasms increases as intensity decreases. Impotence strikes between one-third and one-half of all men by the age of seventy-five.

Women are more fortunate. They do not have to contend with a waiting period between orgasms. Although lubrication diminishes with age, as does the strength of the vaginal walls, maintaining arousal is not a serious problem, and the frequency of orgasm continues.

Aging Americans, however, have not quit trying to enjoy sex. Surgery and implants offer men some relief from impotency, while women can augment lubrication with a simple pharmaceutical solution.

For women, aging may offer additional sexual benefits. More and more older women are reporting an increase in sexual appetites. The onset of menopause and infertility and the resulting freedom from menses and pregnancy may be one reason. And low-dose estrogen replacement therapy can serve to maintain women's sexual interest later in life.

We do know that prior sexual activity best identifies those who will enjoy sexual activity as they age. Young sexually active women become older sexually active women. On the other hand, if sex was not important at nineteen, it probably won't be important at fifty. Aging, however, brings some decline in ability and interest. Sex will be considerably less consuming at the age of forty than it was at nineteen, and even less so at fifty, sixty or seventy.

Sex becomes less hormonally based as we grow older, but a decline in sexual ability is often replaced by an increase in intimacy. Quality rather than quantity becomes the benchmark for enjoyment.

Ageless Energy

What about having the energy to keep up with what we want to do? About half of those over sixty-five experience some sort of sleep disorder, which may affect energy levels. But energy is not intrinsically linked with age, as most people think. In one study, when middle-aged and older (over seventy-five) adults recalled peak high and low energy periods in their lives, both groups reported energy levels peaking somewhere in the forties, and slight declines thereafter. Most said they retained 70 percent of their original energy levels well into their eighties and nineties. When energy levels did decline, those surveyed pinned the deterioration on catastrophic and stressful events, not age.

Those who scored the highest in the energy-level survey were robust eighty-plus country square dancers. They danced several times a week and appeared fairly active. They were alive, eager and vital. Only their physical appearance revealed their chronological ages. Those who were the most energetic also had the most passionate attitudes. As one ninety-year-old noted, "How interested I am in what I'm doing tells me my energy level."

The dancers experienced major declines in energy levels when they suffered a stressful life event. Recovery took approximately two years. When asked to explain their longevity, a group of adults aged ninety and over credited first a healthy lifestyle (47 percent) and then their continued interest in a career or hobby (17 percent).

Neurologist John Meyers studied a healthy group of older adults for four years and found that the most inactive people of this group had poorer blood flow in their brains and fared worse on psychological tests.

We live in a body that ages. But now, for the first time in history, we have opportunities to slow down our rate of physical aging and extend our years in an ageless state.

What is the meaning of all of this? Are we upsetting the natural order of things? Should we try to reverse aging, or should we reconcile ourselves to a gradual and lengthy decline?

12

An Ageless Body?

—

Anything is possible
in a lifetime . . .
even adulthood.

— Howell Raines
from *Fly Fishing Through*
The Midlife Crisis

One day we look in a mirror, and we are disappointedly surprised. We do not expect the gray hair we see, the lines on our faces, like rings inside a tree marking the years. Our bodies are a little more flaccid, despite all-out efforts to trim and tone.

Now that we are emotionally growing up and learning how to be more alive, more true to our own nature, how do we get the physical aging process to slow down? Aging — ugh! It's what Susan Sontag called the *moveable doom* — the continuing reminder of our mortality and lessened appeal.

Why Age At All?

But is age the great leveler it once was? Not anymore. The changes in physical appearance that accompany age are no longer a foregone conclusion, and not everyone is affected to the same degree: each of us ages differently, and our bodily organ systems age at different rates. Although a great deal of aging is in the roll of the genetic dice, some of it seems to be within our control.

Through gerontological discoveries and more attention to mental health, our understanding of increased longevity has quadrupled. Breakthroughs in medical science have moved us closer to asking a previously unthinkable question: Is it is possible to grow up without growing old?

Philosophical considerations aside, we have no idea why we age — we just know that we do and that everything around us does. It all begins quite early — sometime after adolescence — but fortunately our body system prevents us from noticing.

The changes that accompany aging are anything but good: atherosclerosis, menopause, obesity, hypertension, diabetes, immune decline, autoimmune disease, cancers, depression and overreaction to stress. But all is not doom and gloom. Let's understand our genes first.

According to Kathy Keeton, editor of *Longevity* magazine and author of a book with the same title, genes are far more important than we think. There is some freedom from genetics but exactly how much is not certain. In addition, each species has only so much time to carry out evolutionary functions: developing to maturity, mating, producing offspring, parenting.

According to age theory, our DNA — the building block in each living being's gene structure — sets limits for each cell in our bodies. Each cell can divide approximately 50 times before deteriorating. Cells also remember how many times they have divided. For instance, if during laboratory experiments, cells are frozen at twenty-five divisions, they remember they have twenty-five more divisions to go.

The secrets of aging and longevity appear to be linked very strongly to our individual, inherited DNA. It's a complicated subject suitable for scientists and scholars, but the bottom line is that DNA is unmistakably a genetic blueprint both for a given species and for individuals. Genetic theorists have argued that key mechanisms of aging include the ability of certain cells to repair age-damaged DNA. And the fortunate individuals who have genes that are more reparable simply live longer.

The fact that humans have a genetic repair rate twice as fast as that of apes may explain why humans live twice as long.

Our DNA molecules, however, are prone to making errors. When they make a mistake, cross-linking can occur. If cross-linking occurs between relatively harmless cells, we get stiffer and have less flexible bodies. But if the cells cross-link with toxins, then the fats and proteins in our cells become a kind of rust that clogs arteries and causes cataracts and a host of other problems.

Recent work at Rockefeller University, UCLA, Harvard and various research institutes has identified various substances — called antioxidants — that minimize cross-linking within our body. This area of investigation holds great promise in slowing down our aging process.

Longevity

"The trick," writes anthropologist Ashley Montagu, "is simple: to die young as late as possible." When, exactly, physical aging begins and where it will end stumps even the experts. A recent editorial in *Journal Of The American Medical Association* by Stanford University gerontologist James Fries touts the idea of agelessness. Fries writes, "There are increasing data on the ability to move infirmity farther into the lifespan, shortening its overall duration."

Deepak Chopra's *Ageless Body, Timeless Mind* brings quantum medicine into the public awareness. Quantum physics and Indian medicine suggest that we are beginning to push back the effects of time to a point at which the meaning of *old age* becomes much more open to interpretation.

In the United States, if you were a white male born in 1920, your life expectancy at birth was approximately 54.4 years. Your female counterpart could expect to live 55.6 years. A man born in 1960 could expect to live 67.4 years; a woman, 74.1 years. Today men can look forward to living an average of 73.2 years. Women will probably live to be octogenarians. Many will live well into their nineties, and an increasing number will pass the century mark.

Let's hope that when they do, they're better off then the jazz musician who, when interviewed on his 100th birthday, was asked the secret of his longevity. "Hell," he said, "if I'da known I was gonna live this long, I'da took good care of myself."

The increase in longevity shows up in a demographic shift; America is graying. During the next thirty years, 20 percent of Americans will be at least sixty-five-years-old. And the census of 1990 revealed almost 1 million nonagenarians, a 38 percent increase in one decade.

More of us are living longer, and many are living healthier lives. Less than 1 percent of the populaton below the age of seventy-five is to be found in nursing homes. The figure jumps to 20 percent for those in their eighties.

Since longevity statistics include deaths of young people, the older you are, the greater your chances of living far beyond the average life expectancy. If you are a female, and the average life expectancy at the time of your birth was seventy-two, each year that you survive increases your chances of living beyond that marker. For all women alive at the age of forty, the life expectancy might increase to seventy-five years. If you are still here at fifty, then the life expectancy for your age will have increased to about seventy-eight years.

Average Life Expectancy At Different Ages		
	Men	Women
At 70 years old	81.8	85
At 85 years old	90.1	91.3

Although old age is the reported cause of more than 30 percent of all deaths, old age as such never causes death. Most deaths result from the breakdown of some key organ or tissue.

Most people function at their physical peak between eighteen and thirty. Yet in some athletic disciplines, such as weightlifting and long-distance running, for example — people have reported peaks past the age of thirty. Maria Fiatarone, working with nine sedentary older people at Tufts University, found that regular weight-training regimens actually eliminated previous age-related ailments, such as arthritis and muscle weakness. After two months of training, her nine subjects were all physically stronger. None required pain medication.

Cross-Cultural Differences

Aging is also not exactly the same around the world. Heart disease, a disorder generally associated with aging, is not an inevitable consequence of growing older in certain nations. In fact, diet, stress, smoking and exercise are all factors related to heart disease and have more to do with lifestyle than with birthdays.

Medical anthropologists in Venezuela, the Solomon Islands and certain aboriginal tribal areas in Australia have documented low blood pressure in both the oldest and youngest members. The Mbouti of Zaire and the Tara Humara of Mexico have cholesterol counts lower than 150. The !Kung bushmen of the Kalahari Desert suffer little hearing loss. Most primal people never experience our "inevitable" middle-age spread, and, in fact, body fat decreases with age.

I had the opportunity a few years ago to interview people in several primal cultures and found little evidence of what we call aging. The ageless elders of Papua New Guinea are a remarkably lean and active group. Each was made to feel special as a village elder, and those I interviewed had an involved sense of purpose as preservers of culture. Daily activity included at least moderately rigorous exercise. The diet consisted of sap-based bread, supplemented with vegetables; fats were nonexistent. I did not observe much infirmity or dementia.

I made similar observations with regard to the Himalayan cultures of Nepal, Tibet and Bhutan. And other researchers have recorded similar findings with regard to the Russian Abkhasians, the Hunzas of Pakistan, the Japanese Okinawans and the Vilcambas of Equador. Members of these groups live incredibly long lives — well past 100, and the reason appears to be lifestyle. In these communities, life's rhythms are slow and steady, and everyone is made to feel useful. There is also little competition, except in sports and dance. The eldest person is the head of the household, regardless of actual contribution.

The Hunza people, who live in a high mountain valley in the Himalayas, love to play soccer. Their seniors team is reported to be limited to those aged eighty and older.

Longevity is predicated on parents' longevity; relatively high IQ, socioeconomic status, activity level, work satisfaction and active sexuality; and minimal use of alcohol and tobacco. Another factor contributing to longevity, and not usually in the news, is continuity of lifestyle — an orderly routine of eating, working, sex and leisure. Life in primal cultures moves at a slow and steady pace, and regular routines are rarely disrupted even after the age of seventy.

Does a primal lifestyle pay off? It sure does. Where the daily routine consists of regular activity — walking, climbing and lifting — the elderly rarely report back or joint problems. Preventive exercise, rest, weight training, aerobics and other kinds of physical workouts may do much to delay decline in muscle strength and tone. Osteoporosis is dramatically lessened through a regiman of exercise along with a calcium supplement (as well as some hormones) in the diet.

Appearance And Age

Raquel Welch can still pose for swimsuit posters in her fifties. Dick Clark still looks thirty-five. Lena Horne still looks sexy in her seventies. If we are ageless on the inside, adult in our psyches, what about our looks?

People in their forties, fifties, sixties and seventies increasingly look younger than their chronological ages. "I certainly didn't think he was that old," and similar comments, are more and more common.

Aging: What Bothers Men And Women

Problem	Men	Women
Tiring	31%	26%
Wrinkles	6	28
Memory Loss	12	15
Back Problems	19	11
Lowered Sexual Drive	5	4

From *USA Weekend.*

Agelessness And Surgery

Ten years of wrinkles, thirty years of impoverished muscle tone or fifteen years of hair loss can sometimes be reversed with one fell swoop of the knife. Cosmetic surgeries are growing in number and type. There are tummy tucks, facelifts, breast implants and hair transplants. Between 1981 and 1988, 100,000 of us have had liposuction to remove fat; 80,000 of us have had our eyes surgically altered to look more youthful; approximately 70,000 have had nose jobs and breast augmentations. Facelifts number 50,000 (91 percent women), tummy tucks number 20,000 (91 percent women) and hair transplants number 3,188.

Besides the designer services that snip, tuck, push and pull back the years, surgery also includes replacing parts. An estimated 2 million Americans became more functional with artificial arms, arteries, elbow joints, heart valves and other parts. Each year about 1.2 million receive eye lense implants, 122,000 receive pacemakers and 250,000 receive artificial hips.

We live in bodies that age, but through a variety of circumstances. For the first time in history, we have opportunities to slow down aging and move into physiologically ageless aging — able to maintain vigorous physical health and a relatively youthful appearance — nearly until the end of our lifespan.

Then what will aging mean? Will younger people continue to get up and give their seats on the bus to seniors? Will seniors still be given discounts at restaurants? Will there continue to be a legal age of retirement?

And if our ability to retard aging continues, will we ultimately be able to eliminate a finite lifespan altogether? If so, will we be forced to restrict human births so as not to multiply ourselves to death? Would we, as a society, legally limit the number of years anyone is allowed to live?

And if there were no feebleness in old age, might our society revert to an attitude of respect for elders, and come to understand that growing old is truly growing?

13

Meaningful Adulthood

—

*I wanted only
to try to live in accord
with the promptings which
came from my true self.
Why was that so
very difficult?*

— Hermann Hesse
from *Demian*

W hy does it take us so long to realize who we are? Why is it so difficult to determine what we really need? Why do we spend so much time focusing on the trees instead of the forest? In short, what really matters to us?

It has been stated that the shift to true adulthood is a transition from cultural to personal meaning. Norma, a fifty-nine-year-old mother and grandmother, echoes a common experience:

> *I grew up on the farm back in Arkansas and raised eight children. Don't ask me why I had eight children, I have no idea. We were good Catholics and I thought it was the thing to do, I guess. My husband was abusive at times but I couldn't leave . . . and we had no money of course. So I threw myself into my kids. Now the last one is still home and I think I resent him being there. He's thirty and he's going to a counselor. He's on drugs. I want him to leave, but he's got no job and nowhere to go. At this point I just want to pack my bags and go back to Arkansas. I don't care if I got to go on Welfare. Now I want this time for me!*

Norma had been living the life dictated to her by the prevailing culture. At fifty-nine, she saw that, until then, her emotional life had been like a sieve that only every so often permitted something that mattered to slip through.

Now for the first time in her life, she had the opportunity to remove the sieve and let the essential part rush through. Norma was ready to shift to personal meaning, to move into emotional adulthood.

What Is Meaningful?

Meaningful experiences can be said to fall into three categories: religious, metaphysical and existential. For some it is a divinity that gives meaning to their experience; for others it is an impersonal face; and for still others it is the very experience itself that is meaningful.

From whatever point of view individuals seek meaning and in whatever context they find it, they seem to be able to identify the kernal of meaning in experiences that really mattered to them!

Curiosity about how individuals define what matters led me to conduct several hundred interviews with a variety of persons from settings across several cultures. I wanted to know what mattered to a dentist, to a store manager, to a laborer and to homeless people. I searched high and low for the commonalities in their life stories. I found for the most part, the following features:

- Most meaningful experiences occurred before the age of forty.
- Most people had experienced three or four meaningful events in a liftetime.
- Most people defined the events in terms of emotional salience.

Meaningful events appeared to focus on survival, cultural compliance or individual experience; the most important factor in making the experience meaningful seemed to be emotional salience. Whatever experiences were named, they were imbued with high emotions that fitted into an overall life pattern and revealed the makeup and artistry of the person.

Let's return to Norma. Here was a woman who had not been living psychologically, who had lived in accordance with cultural expectations. She was fifty-nine and for the first time ready to make the transition to full emotional adulthood. Previously, her children had been all that had mattered to her. Why?

It is my belief that Norma's children (1) forced her to become emotionally invested, (2) focused her will or sense of purpose and (3) made her actively involved with others in her environment. It is my belief that it is these three elements — passion, will, connection — that make experiences matter.

Paul, forty-eight, from London, England, formerly did a little of everything. He was a builder, a carpenter, a hang-gliding pilot. Now he travels the world painting landscapes and making frames for artists.

> It's not work anymore, it's play that's the difference with what I'd call my devotional art form. I'm trying to make every aspect of my life understand art work, in taking part in the creative process. It's what self-determines. I don't really have separate meaningful events per se, I'm sort of at peace with myself. I'm happy. For a while, I had that mid-life crisis, or whatever you call it. But I've emerged triumphant. I'm starting to get what I've been missing. I guess you'd say I'm experiencing the presence of the Creator moment by moment.

For Paul, true adulthood and living a meaningful life went hand in hand.

Jonathan offers another picture of an emotional adult in transition. At twenty-eight, this quiet and shy banking analyst from Melbourne, Australia, married an American woman and tried his hand on Wall Street. Buying corporate bonds and investing for a major bank didn't work for him. Ulcers, drinking and insomnia amounted to too big a price to pay for success, and his disillusionment began:

*New York. I couldn't handle it. It's a crazy scene there.
Nobody gets close to anybody. Well, I shouldn't say that. I
got close to three others, and they were fired, and another
got transferred to Switzerland. I had enough . . . the ulcers,
and I started drinking at age twenty-six. So I quit. I'm back
to myself again. But, now I don't know what to do. I'm like
a vagabond, my wife says. I don't know. Maybe I'm just
trying to figure out who I really am for the first time.*

*The thing that stands out the most has to do with my
time with Ian Stapleton. A remarkable chap, Stapleton has
sworn off material wealth in order to offer kids a new way
of thinking. Every day he takes inner city kids into the
camp up in the Victorian Alps — beautiful — to a place he
built, an outdoor school that he started. He's the most down-
to-earth man I know. Honest and living the life he wants.*

For Jonathan, adulthood was to begin with a search for
a career that mattered. Life elsewhere isn't so malleable,
especially in those cultures that thwart independence of
thought and action in favor of extensive cultural complicity.

Such is the experience of Ugyen, Jonathan's counterpart
in the Himalayas. Ugyen Rinzing, also twenty-eight, is a
tour operator in Thimpu, Bhutan. Ugyen is married and
has a child. He shared these experiences:

*When I finished my studies, I had to come back to Bhutan
to look after my parents. I have sisters who do the same. We
are taught to stand on our own two feet at a very young age.
My parents are alive but very old; so now it is my duty to
take care of them.*

*I come from a family that cared little for education. One
of the most meaningful events was that I remember arguing
with them that I wished to be sent to school. I don't think
that they valued it but I kept arguing and arguing and
eventually they sent me to Calcutta for an education. If not
for that, I wouldn't be where I am today. The other thing
that stands out was in the tenth grade and the realization
that I had about understanding the world. For ten years, I
was in a British insititution of learning in India and we*

were taught their way of understanding the world. When I
returned to Bhutan, I opened up my mind to the Buddhist
as well as the Christian concepts. It made quite a difference
to open me up.

For Ugyen, the road to true emotional adulthood is
much more difficult than for Jonathan or Paul. He has to
fight not only himself but also a system in which his kind
of thinking is not understood as part of a natural adult
development.

Papua New Guinea is even less tolerant than Bhutan.
There is absolutely no deviation from religion and the
dominant culture. Wut, who reports his current age as
"some time in eighties," explains:

Adult. I am an old man now. I was an adult as a young
man when I go through initiation. What matters most? Ah
. . . when I was small boy, the aboriginals took me away
and I had to stay with them for a long time. A crocodile got
me, and I was almost killed [he shows scars on his stomach]
and then, a snake bit me, and I almost died. I am telling you
this as it is.

For Wut, survival and the triumph over adversity is
primarily meaningful — and it is closely allied with the
primary rite of initiation. Had he not gone through the
bleeding and scarring ritual, he might not have felt like an
adult and would have been treated as a lesser person by
his peers.

A Culture Of Meaning

Can we create a truly adult, age-free, meaningful culture? According to romantics, the answer is yes, but I am
not convinced. As of now, it is certainly unsafe to reveal
your agelessness, your passion and your playfulness except in very limited places and circumstances. Only when
it is truly safe can we shift to a more meaningful perspec-

tive and be ourselves. André offers his social criticism to dining partner Wally in the film *My Dinner With André*:

> *I think New York is the new model for the new concentration camp, where the camp has been built by the inmates and the inmates are guards and they have this pride in this thing that they've built, they've built their own prison. And so, they exist in a state of schizophrenia where they are both the guards and the prisoners. And as a result, they no longer have (having been lobotomized) the capacity to leave the prison they've made or even to see it as a prison.*

Social visionary Max Weber thought along the same lines. Predicting industrial fallout, Weber feared that we would all become hollow, mechanized zombies, contemporary counterparts of Charlie Chaplin in the movie *Modern Times*, endlessly going through in the prescribed motions even when released from the production line.

The "blahs" — rare in primitive cultures — represent a common consequence of daily living in our postindustrial society. And in response modern psychiatry has built up an arsenal for combatting the blahs, as the popularity of Prozac and other mood elevators reach unprecedented levels.

Years ago psychoanalyst Karen Horney addressed the problem of emotional adulthood and society:

> *At the core of this alienation from the actual self is a phenomenon that is less tangible although more crucial. It is the remoteness of the neurotic from his own feelings, wishes, beliefs and energies. It is the loss of the feeling of being an active determining force in his own life. It is the loss of feeling himself as an organic whole. These in turn indicate an alienation from that most alive center of ourselves which I have suggested calling the real self. To present more fully its propensities in the terms of William James: it provides the "palpitating inward life"; it engenders the spontaneity of feelings, whether these be joy, yearning, love, anger, fear, despair. It also is the source of spontaneous interest and*

*energies, the source of effort and attention from which ema-
nate the fiats of will; the capacity to wish and will; it is the
part of ourselves that wants to expand and grow and to
fulfill itself.*

At the time Horney wrote — more than half a century
ago — nobody listened. Instead history pegged her as a
Freudian revisionist. History was also cruel to James,
whose efforts nearly a century ago to work out a psychology based on associations were vastly overshadowed by
Freud's work on the unconscious mind. But their theories
now mesh perfectly with our notion of agelessness — an
idea whose time has come at last.

APPENDIX

Features Of Transition To Adulthood

- *Clinical Features:* Anxiety, depression, sleep disorders, constant worrying, fatigue, chronic depersonalization or derealization. Individuals report being "in a fog." Alternatively, there is an integration of emotions and cognitions to produce a change in awareness and perception of self and others. An enhanced sense of self upon completion of the tripartite phase.

- *Age Of Onset:* Two studies have found that people commonly report age of onset to occur approximately at age thirty. But because transition has been observed to occur at all ages it is apparently not age related.

- *Sex Ratio:* Unrelated to sex. Men appear to "act out" more; women tend to become more depressed.

- *Ethnicity/Culture:* Collectivist cultures are at risk for delay as are cultures which restrict individuality.

- *Course:* One study has found a developmental shift/crisis which averages 2.8 years, and can be completed as early as 1.5 years and as late as 5 years.

- *Impairment:* There may be moderate impairment in social functioning, most notably a withdrawal from social relations followed by a change of friends.

- *Complications:* Marital stresses increase dramatically because the spouse does not comprehend the nature and extent of the changes which are occurring. Difficulties at work such as a shift in attitude toward superiors or peers is also common.

- *Predisposing Factors For Onset:* Awareness of emotional needs and feelings.

- *Predisposing Factors For Delay:* Emotional overprotection, defense mechanism of denial, compulsive disorders such as workaholism, drug or alcohol dependency and severe character disorders.

- *Prevalence:* Unknown. There is no research on the percentage of people who work through metamorphosis to achieve true adulthood.

- *Usual Diagnosis:* Depression. Adjustment disorder. Existential crisis. Clinicians may attribute the symptoms to depression, anxiety or a "phase of life" disorder caused by a crisis, such as divorce.

GLOSSARY

Generations: Baby Boomers, Baby Busters, Generation 'X', etc.

A group of people born at a specific period in time, usually the same decade, who share the same historical experience such as baby boomers, baby busters and Depression-era. Often confused with aging differences, birth into a particular generation is a cultural designation and has little or no influence on the emotional life of an individual person. There are no consistent research findings for generational influence on personality.

True/Emotional Adulthood

The psychological process of shifting from a cultural to an emotional base. All that an individual believed and did which was culturally meaningful shifts in priority to the background in favor of things, events, and people that personally and emotionally matter. This true adulthood has no direct bearing on the biological, chronological or the cultural impact of menopause or a midpoint in the lifespan.

Maturation

Formerly defined by cultural-based behavioral standards of social responsibility and autonomy. Now maturation must also include the internal changes that accompany emotional adulthood.

Menopause

A biologically based definition of the end of reproduction with strong cultural and psychological overlay. The average age of onset is fifty with a seven-year range before or after. This average age is not universal and occurs much earlier in pre-industrial cultures. In addition, there is research to suggest psychological and personality differences in individuals, such as findings that emotionally labile women have greater sensitivity to hot flashes than calmer women. At this writing, there is no acknowledged male menopause since it is believed that men are less hormonally dependent.

Middle age or midlife

This is chronologically based and culturally defined. Since people are living well into their eighties, middle age or midlife is generally agreed upon to begin at age forty and extend approximately to age sixty-five, when old age is thought to begin. An exact definition is difficult since very few cultures have an acknowledged midlife phase to the life cycle and longevity keeps pushing back the endpoint. What midlife or a midpoint was at the turn of the century is qualitatively and quantitatively different from today's definitions. Culture-bound definitions begin as early as thirty and as late as sixty. In our culture, most individuals agree on about age forty-five, although others base it on an event such as menopause. This term should not be confused with the "midlife crisis."

CHAPTER NOTES

Introduction

Page Number

xv   Gerzon, M. (January 1990). Starting over at mid-life. *Utne Reader*, p. 70.

1. Adulthood: What Is It? Where Is It?

9   Erikson, E. (1950). *Childhood and society*. New York: Norton.

2. Culture And Life's Stages

14   Oldenburg, D. (October 19, 1991). Fifty-five-year-olds find themselves. *Detroit News*, p. 5C.

14   Brokaw, T. Turning fifty. *New York Times Magazine*, p. 17.

19   Cohen, R. (May 1987). Suddenly I'm the adult. *Psychology Today*, p. 70.

23   Iyer, P. (1991). *The lady and the monk*. New York: Knopf, p. 100. Also see Halper, J. (1988). *Quiet desperation*. New York: Warner.

3. Growing Pains

28   Erikson, E. (1950). *Childhood and society*. New York: Norton.

29   Levinson, D., et al. (1978). *The seasons of a man's life*. New York: Ballantine, p. 57.

30   Vaillant, G. (1977). *Adaptation to life*. Boston: Little, Brown, p. 80.

30   Gould, R. (1978). *Transformations*. New York: Simon and Schuster. It is uncertain what defines adulthood/midlife. One idea was greater preoccupation with death. Freudians have no evidence to empirically support Jacques's well accepted notion that at midlife there is an increased preoccupation with death anxiety. (See Baum, S. & Boxley, R. (1984). Age denial: Death denial in the elderly. *Death Education*, 8, pp. 419-423.) Then came Erikson who, too, enjoyed widespread acceptance despite no evidence to support his theory in whole. Eriksonian stages appear to reflect Western culture's notion of success, and do not hold up cross-culturally as true development should. (See Paul Roazen's (1976). Erik Erikson, New York Free Press). Gerontologists at times fare no better. Let us use the often cited Grant study (Vaillant 1977) for example. At Harvard, Vaillant found that men who married and had children had more successful outcomes than those who did not, lending support to the intimacy and generativity notions of Eriksonian theory. But the outcome did not examine such details as marital satisfaction, number of children required to achieve generativity, or why both "successful" and "unsuccessful" individuals had been in psychotherapy or counseling. The study was completed in the 1960's using that era's value system as a standard for intimacy, generativity and ego integrity. And by the 1990's, using that era's value system as a standard for intimacy, generativity, and ego integrity, gerontology's ideas of what constituted successful outcome had changed. On the other hand there is some support for Levinson's theory of the "age thirty" crisis (Roberts, P. & Newton, P. (1987). Levinsonian studies of women's adult development. *Psychology and Aging*, 2, pp. 154-163.) but

really not much backing for other elements of his theory (Hedlund, B. & Ebersole, P. (1983). A test of Levinson's mid-life re-evaluation. *Journal of Genetic Psychology*, 143, pp. 189-192; Merriam, S. (1983). Mentors and proteges: A critical review of the literature. *Adult Education Quarterly*, 33, pp. 161-173). To date, Gould (1978) offers the most psychologically sophisticated work.

31   Loevinger, J. (1976). *Ego development*. San Francisco: Jossey-Bass.

31   Kegan, R. (1982). *The evolving self*. Cambridge, MA: Harvard University.

31   Stein, M. (1983). *In midlife*. Dallas: Spring, p. 23, regarding the uncanny or unheimlickkeit.

32   Brim, G. (1992). New perspectives on midlife development. Paper presented at the 25th International Congress of Psychology, Brussels. Hardliner M/DMAC researchers report only 5 percent of the population has internal upheavals. See (May 1993). Midlife myths. *Atlantic*.

32   McCrae, R. & Costa, P. (1984). Emerging lives, enduring dispositions. Boston: Little, Brown.

32   Gallup poll reported 27 percent. In other studies 50 percent report a "crisis." See Andrea Graber's doctoral dissertation: Female life-span development (1991). For more stability or change arguments see Paul Costa, Ravena Heison or better yet, see Michael Apted's BBC documentary series 35 Up.

4. Metamorphosis: Shift, Storm And Homeward Bound

44   Cohen, R. (May 1987). Suddenly I'm the adult. *Psychology Today*, p. 70.

48   Gould, J. (January 27, 1991). The virtues of virtue. *New York Times Magazine*, p. 12.

49   Goldsmith, J. (May 1987). Suddenly I'm the adult. *Op cit.*

50   Whitbourne, S. (1986). *The me I know*. New York: Springer-Verlag.

52   Blumenthal, M. (May/June 1992). LSD at midlife. *New Age Journal,* p. 146.

54   Plaskin, G. (1992). *Turning points.* New York: Birch Lane.

55   Howard, J. & Wagenheim, J. (July/August 1993). Men at midlife. *New Age Journal,* p. 54.

56   Personal communication, Toronto, 1987.

59   Personal communication, Los Angeles, 1994.

62   Also see Gilligan, C. (1982). *In a different voice.* Cambridge, MA: Harvard University; Rubin, L. (1979). *Women of a certain age.* New York: Harper Colophon; Belenky, M.F., Clinchy, B.M., Goldberger, N.R. & Tarule, J.M. (1986). *Women's ways of knowing.* New York: Basic.

63   Becker, E. (1973). *The denial of death.* New York: Free Press.

65   Gerzon, M. (1992). *Coming into our own.* New York: Delacorte.

66   Turkel, S. (1992). *Race.* New York: New Press.

5. Adult Self-Appraisal

70   Under revision with validity and reliability coefficients soon available.

6. When They're Gone

82   Palmerston, V. (October 7, 1990). Up north. *Detroit Free Press,* p. 22.

83   Lovenheim, B. (1990). *Beating the marriage odds.* New York: Morrow.

83   David Olson, Ph.D., research of over 15,000 couples at the University of Minnesota found seven "types" of marriages. 1. Devitalized (40%); 2. Financial (11%); 3. Conflicted (14%); 4. Traditional (10%); 5. Balanced (8%); 6. Harmonious (8%); 7. Vitalized (9%), as reported in (1993) An arrangement of marriages. *Psychology Today,* p. 22.

85   The "American dream" revised statistics from Bureau of the Census. (1987). *Statistical abstract of the United States.* Washington, D.C.: Superintendent of Documents. U.S. Government Printing Office, p. 3421.

7. Grown-ups Who Don't Grow Up

94   Masson, J. (1990). *Final analysis.* Reading, MA: Addison-Wesley.

95   Werblin, J.M. (May/June 1992). Glorious Ms. Steinem. *Changes,* p. 41.

8. The Spirit And Adulthood

104   Jung, C. (1965). *Memories, dreams and reflections.* New York: Vintage Books.

107   Ader, R. (Ed.) (1981). *Psychoimmunology.* New York: Academic.

107   Diamond, M., Johnson, R., Protti, A., Ott, C. & Kajisa, L. (1985). Plasticity in the 904-day-old male rat cerebral cortex. *Experimental Neurology,* 87, pp. 309-337.

107   Erikson, E., Erikson, J. & Kivnick, H. (1986). *Vital involvement in old age.* New York: W.W. Norton.

107   (May 1992). The war on aging and disease: a status report. *Longevity,* pp. 28-39.

110   Brewster, T. (June 1991). Lee Atwater's last campaign. *Reader's Digest,* p. 119.

9. The Soul Has No Age

116   Nozick, R. (1989). *The examined life.* Touchstone, p. 23. Also see Karp, D. (1988). A decade of reminders: change age consciousness between fifty and sixty years old. *Gerontologist,* 28, pp. 727-738.

117   Davis, I. (December 29, 1991). Age before beauty. *New York Times Magazine.*

118   Baum, S. & Boxley, R. (1983). Age identification in the elderly. *Gerontologist,* 23, pp. 532-537.

118   Rubenstein, C. (May 1991). The new adulthood. *Glamour,* p. 281.

119   Previous researchers believed that "younger feeling" elderly were denying their age. Terms such as "illusionary misperception" and theorizing that "bodily changes threat-

en identity" and cause "an inherent difficulty in modifying one's body precept" still maintain their hold (Perry, S. (1989). The phantom self of middle-age, in Oldham, J.M. & Liebert, R. S. *The middle years*. New Haven: Yale University, p. 196). Even some gerontologist believe that ". . . seeing oneself as younger may be a denial of reality, but a denial that may be necessary for good psychological functioning." (Linn, M. & Hunter, K. (1979). Perception of age in the elderly. *Journal of Gerontology*, 34, pp. 46-53). Today it is better understood that "younger feeling" elderly are simply healthier, happier and essentially "age-free." (Baum, S. (1983). Age identification in the elderly. Some theoretical considerations. *International Journal of Aging and Human Development*, 18, pp. 23-30).

122   de Beauvoir, S. (1972). *The coming of age*. New York: Warner.

122   Grotjahn, M. (1982). The day I got old. *Psychiatric Clinics of North America*, 5, p. 233. See also Hebb, D. (November 1986). On watching myself get old. *Psychology Today*.

125   Morgan, T. (May 1987). What does a 60-year-old man see when he looks in the mirror? *Esquire*, p. 161.

10. New Age Aging

128   Neugarten, B. (May 1987). The changing meaning of age. *Psychology Today*, p. 30.

128   Herz, S. American Psychological Association, Annual Convention, 1987, Toronto.

129   Updike, J. (1918). *Rabbit at rest*. New York: Knopf.

130   (September 9, 1992). Age. *Detroit Free Press*, p. 81.

131   Sherrill, R. (July 1992). The truth about growing old. *Esquire*, p. 51. See also (September 9, 1992). Norman Vaughn, act your age. *Outside*, p. 72.

132   Lovenheim, B. (1990). *Beating the marriage odds*. New York: Morrow. An interesting study was carried out by Laurel Klinger-Vartabedian in Amarillo, Texas with Lauren Wiaspe of the University of Oklahoma. When census data of women aged fifty to seventy-four was analyzed for age of spouse and death rates, the following trend was

observed: Among women who had husbands six to fourteen years younger, 30 percent lived longer than expected.
Same-aged women lived 14 percent longer and women
who had husbands six or more years older died 67 percent
sooner).

133   Atchely, R. quoted in the *Sacramento Bee*, January 2, 1991,
p. D4. In a related study, "old age" began at seventy-one
in one poll taken in the 1970's and today is thought to
occur at age seventy-nine. (*Wall Street Journal*, December
31, 1991).

134   Brecher, M. and the eds. of Consumer Reports. (1984).
Love, sex and aging. Consumer Union of the United States.

135   Huzinga, J. (1955). *Homo Ludens.* Boston: Beacon.

11. The Body Electric

145   (May 1992). The war on aging and disease: a status report. *Longevity*, pp. 28-39.

145   *Ibid.*

145   *Op. cit.*

148   (December 1984). Can we slow the inevitable? *Discover*,
p. 17.

149   *Op. cit.*

149   (June 12, 1991). *Detroit Free Press*, p. 18.

150   (August 23, 1993). A genetic clue to Alzheimer's disease.
Newsweek, p. 44.

150   (January 1991). Centrophenoxine combination of DMAE
and auxin. *Longevity*, p. 40.

152   Temoshok, L. & Dreher, H. (1993). *The type C connection.*
New York: NAL.

152   *Op. cit.*

154   *Op. cit.*

12. An Ageless Body?

157   Keeton, K. (1992). *Longevity.* New York: Viking.

158   (May 1992). The war on aging and disease: a status report. *Longevity*, pp. 28-39.

158   Fries, J. (January 19, 1990). The sunny side of aging. *Journal of the American Medical Association*, 263, p. 2354.

158   Chopra, D. (1993). *Ageless body, timeless mind*. New York: Harmony Books.

160   *Op. cit.*

162   (December 29, 1989). *USA Weekend*, p. 5.

162   (March 1990). In Health, p. 12. Actual facelift number is 48,480.

13. Meaningful Adulthood

170   Shawn, W. & Gregory, A. (1981). *My dinner with Andre*. New York: Grove, p. 93. For other related work see Sherman, E. (1987). *Meaning in mid-life transition*. Albany: State University of New York and Stern, A. (1971). *The search for meaning*. Memphis: Memphis State University.

READING LIST

Doi, T. (1986). *The anatomy of self*. Tokyo: Kodansha International.

Fromm, E. (1955). *The sane society*. New York: Rinehart.

Fromm, E. (1968). *The revolution of hope*. New York: Bantam.

Gerzon, M. (1992). *Coming into our own*. New York: Delacorte.

Gould, R. (1978). *Transformations*. New York: Simon and Schuster.

Hancock, E. (1989). *The girl within*. New York: Fawcett Columbine.

Horney, K. (1950). *Neurosis and human growth*. New York: W.W. Norton & Co.

Kegan, R. (1982). *The evolving self*. Cambridge, MA: Harvard University.

Leonard, L. (1985). *The wounded woman*. Boston: Shambhala.

Levinson, D. (1979). *The seasons of a man's life*. New York: Ballantine.

Modell, A. (1993). *The private self.* Cambridge, MA: Harvard University.

Montagu, A. (1981). *Growing young.* New York: McGraw-Hill.

Stein, M. (1983). *In midlife.* Dallas: Spring.

Whitbourne, S. (1986). *The me I know.* New York: Springer-Verlag.

Winnicott, D.W. (1965). *The maturational process and the facilitating environment.* New York: International Universities.

Vaillant, G. (1977). *Adaptation to life.* Boston: Little, Brown.

Books To Set Your Spirit Free

Chicken Soup For The Soul
101 Stories To Open The Heart And Rekindle The Spirit
Jack Canfield and Mark Victor Hansen

Here is a treasury of 101 stories collected by two of America's best-loved inspirational speakers. Metaphors for life's deep and profound truths, these stories provide models for what is possible, give us permission to be more fully human, and illuminate and clarify the path we walk. Just what the doctor ordered to heal your soul and put a smile on your face.

Code 262X (paperback) $12.00
Code 2913 (cloth) $20.00

Acts Of Kindness
How To Create A Kindness Revolution
Meladee McCarty and Hanoch McCarty

The long-overdue kindness revolution is sweeping the country and is waiting for you to enlist! This delightful book tells you everything you need to know to perform intentional acts of kindness for your family, friends, co-workers, schoolmates, strangers and people in need. With ideas and directions for over 100 heartwarming things to do, you'll never run out of ways to spread sunshine.

Code 2956 .... $10.00

3201 S.W. 15th Street
Deerfield Beach, FL 33442-8190
1-800-441-5569

Health Communications, Inc.®